About the Authors

Scott Empson is the associate chair of the Bachelor of Applied Information Systems Technology degree program at the Northern Alberta Institute of Technology in Edmonton, Alberta, Canada, where he teaches Cisco routing, switching, and network design courses in a variety of different programs—certificate, diploma, and applied degree—at the postsecondary level. Scott also is the program coordinator of the Cisco Networking Academy Program at NAIT, a Regional Academy covering central and northern Alberta. He has earned three undergraduate degrees: a bachelor of arts, with a major in English; a bachelor of education, again with a major in English/language arts; and a bachelor of applied information systems technology, with a major in network management. Scott currently is completing his master of education from the University of Portland. He holds several industry certifications, including CCNP, CCAI, Network+, and CIEH. Prior to instructing at NAIT, he was a junior/senior high school English/language arts/computer science teacher at different schools throughout Northern Alberta. Scott lives in Edmonton, Alberta, with his wife, Trina, and two children, Zachariah and Shaelyn.

Hans Roth is an instructor in the Electrical Engineering Technology department at Red River College in Winnipeg, Manitoba, Canada. Hans has been with the college for 13 years and teaches in both the engineering technology and IT areas. He has been with the Cisco Networking Academy since 2000, teaching CCNP curricula. Previous to teaching, Hans spent 15 years in R&D/product development designing microcontroller-based control systems for consumer products as well as for the automotive and agricultural industries.

About the Technical Reviewer

Rick Graziani teaches computer science and computer networking courses at Cabrillo College in Aptos, California. Rick has worked and taught in the computer networking and information technology field for almost 30 years. Prior to teaching, Rick worked in IT for various companies, including Santa Cruz Operation, Tandem Computers, and Lockheed Missiles and Space Corporation. He holds an M.A. in computer science and systems theory from California State University Monterey Bay. Rick also does consulting work for Cisco Systems and other companies. When Rick is not working, he is most likely surfing. Rick is an avid surfer who enjoys surfing at his favorite Santa Cruz breaks.

Dedications

This book is again dedicated to my wonderful family, Trina, Zach, and Shae. Working on these books as well as my master's classes took me away from you all too often, and I thank you for all of your love and support.

—Scott

I'd like to thank my wife, Carol, and daughter, Tess, for their constant support and understanding during those times I've spent cloistered in the basement writing.

—Hans

Acknowledgments

Anyone who has ever had anything to do with the publishing industry knows that it takes many, many people to create a book. Our names might be on the cover, but there is no way that we can take credit for all that occurred to get this book from idea to publication.

From Scott Empson: To the team at Cisco Press, once again you amaze me with your professionalism and the ability to make me look good. Mary Beth, Chris, Patrick, Drew, Bill, and Dayna—thank you for your continued support and belief in my little engineering journal.

Also with Cisco Press, a huge thank you to the marketing and publicity staff—Kourtnaye, Doug, and Jamie, as well as Kristin, Curt, and Emily. Without your hard work, no one would even know about these books, and for that I thank you (as does my wife and her credit card companies).

To my technical reviewer, Rick Graziani—thanks for keeping me on track and making sure that what I wrote was correct and relevant. I have known you for many years through the Cisco Networking Academy, and now I finally have had a chance to work with you. I hope I've lived up to your standards.

A big thank you goes to my co-author, Hans Roth, for helping me through this with all of your technical expertise and willingness to assist in trying to make my ideas a reality.

From Hans Roth: The writing part of this process is only the tip of the iceberg. The overall effort is large and the involvement is wide to get any book completed. Working with you folks at Cisco Press has again been a wonderful partnership. Your ongoing professionalism, understanding, and patience have consistently helped me do a little better each time I sit down to write. Thank you, Mary Beth, Chris, Patrick, Drew, and Dayna.

To the technical reviewer, Rick Graziani, thank you for your clarifications and questions.

Thank you, Scott, for your positive approach and energy, your attention to technical detail, your depth of expertise, as well as your "let's do it now!" method. It's always a great pleasure to try to keep up with you.

Contents at a Glance

Contents

Icons Used in This Book

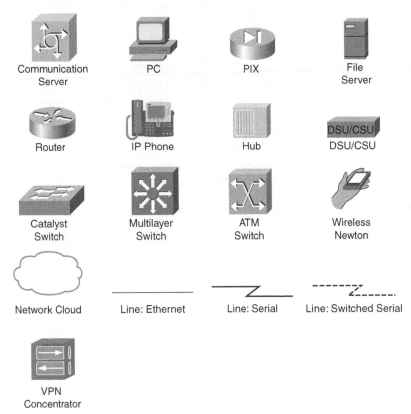

Communication Server

PC

PIX

File Server

Router

IP Phone

Hub

DSU/CSU

Catalyst Switch

Multilayer Switch

ATM Switch

Wireless Newton

Network Cloud

Line: Ethernet

Line: Serial

Line: Switched Serial

VPN Concentrator

Command Syntax Conventions

The conventions used to present command syntax in this book are the same conventions used in the IOS Command Reference. The Command Reference describes these conventions as follows:

- **Boldface** indicates commands and keywords that are entered literally as shown. In actual configuration examples and output (not general command syntax), boldface indicates commands that are manually input by the user (such as a **show** command).
- *Italic* indicates arguments for which you supply actual values.
- Vertical bars (|) separate alternative, mutually exclusive elements.
- Square brackets ([ ]) indicate an optional element.
- Braces ({ }) indicate a required choice.
- Braces within brackets ([{ }]) indicate a required choice within an optional element.

Introduction

Welcome to *CCNP ROUTE Portable Command Guide*! When Cisco Press approached me about updating the four-volume *CCNP Portable Command Guides*, two thoughts immediately jumped into my head: "Is it time for revisions already?" and "Yikes! I am in the middle of pursuing my master's degree. Where will I find the time?" Because of those thoughts, two more soon followed: "I wonder what Hans is up to?" and "I hope Carol is in a good mood, as I am about to ask to take Hans away again...." The result is what you now have before you; a new *Portable Command Guide* for the latest version of the CCNP exam that focuses on routing: CCNP ROUTE.

For those of you who have worked with my books before, thank you for looking at this one. I hope that it will help you as you prepare for the vendor exam, or assist you in your daily activities as a Cisco network administrator/manager. For those of you who are new to my books, you are reading what is essentially a cleaned-up version of my own personal engineering journals—a small notebook that I carry around with me that contains little nuggets of information; commands that I use but then forget; IP address schemes for the parts of the network I work with only occasionally; and quick refreshers for those concepts that I work with only once or twice a year. Although I teach these topics to postsecondary students, the classes I teach sometimes occur only once a year; as you can attest to, it is extremely difficult to remember all those commands all the time. Having a journal of commands at your fingertips, without having to search the Cisco website, can be a real time-saver (or a job-saver if the network is down and you are responsible for getting it back online).

With the creation of the new CCNP exam objectives, there is always something new to read; or a new podcast to listen to; or another slideshow from Cisco Live that you missed or want to review. The engineering journal can be that central repository of information that won't weigh you down as you carry it from the office or cubicle to the server and infrastructure rooms in some remote part of the building or some branch office.

To make this guide a more realistic one for you to use, the folks at Cisco Press have decided to continue with an appendix of blank pages—pages on which you can write your own personal notes, such as your own configurations, commands that are not in this book but are needed in your world, and so on. That way, this book will look less like the authors' journals and more like your own.

Networking Devices Used in the Preparation of This Book

To verify the commands that are in this new series of *CCNP Portable Command Guides*, many different devices were used. The following is a list of the equipment used in the preparation of these books:

- C2620 router running Cisco IOS Release 12.3(7)T, with a fixed Fast Ethernet interface, a WIC 2A/S serial interface card, and an NM-1E Ethernet interface
- C2811 ISR bundle with PVDM2, CMME, a WIC-2T, FXS and FXO VICs, running Cisco IOS Release 12.4(3g)

- C2821 ISR bundle with HWICD 9ESW, a WIC 2A/S, running 12.4(16) Advanced Security IOS
- WS-C3560-24-EMI Catalyst Switch, running Cisco IOS Release 12.2(25)SE
- WS-C3550-24-EMI Catalyst Switch, running Cisco IOS Release 12.1(9)EA1c
- WS-2960-24TT-L Catalyst Switch, running Cisco IOS Release 12.2(25)SE
- WS-2950-12 Catalyst Switch, running version C2950-C3.0(5.3)WC(1) Enterprise Edition Software
- WS-C3750-24TS Catalyst Switches, running ipservicesk9 release 12.2(52)SE
- C1760-V Voice Router with PVDM-256K-20, WIC-4ESW, VIC-2FXO, VIC-2FXS running ENTSERVICESK9 release 12.4(11)T2

You might notice that some of the devices were not running the latest and greatest IOS. Some of them are running code that is quite old.

Those of you familiar with Cisco devices will recognize that a majority of these commands work across the entire range of the Cisco product line. These commands are not limited to the platforms and IOS versions listed. In fact, in most cases, these devices are adequate for someone to continue their studies beyond the CCNP level as well. We have endeavored to identify throughout the book commands that are specific to a platform and/or IOS version.

Who Should Read This Book?

This book is for those people preparing for the CCNP ROUTE exam, whether through self-study, on-the-job training and practice, study within the Cisco Academy Program, or study through the use of a Cisco Training Partner. This book includes some handy hints and tips along the way to make life a bit easier for you in this endeavor. It is small enough that you will find it easy to carry around with you. Big, heavy textbooks might look impressive on your bookshelf in your office, but can you really carry them all around with you when you are working in some server room or equipment closet somewhere?

Strategies for Exam Preparation

The strategy that you use for CCNP ROUTE might be slightly different from strategies that other readers use, mainly based on the skills, knowledge, and experience you already have obtained. For instance, if you have attended the ROUTE course, you might take a different approach than someone who learned routing via on-the-job training. Regardless of the strategy you use or the background you have, the book is designed to help you get to the point where you can pass the exam with the least amount of time required. For instance, there is no need for you to practice or read about EIGRP or OSPF if you fully understand it already. However, many people like to make sure that they truly know a topic and thus read over material that they already know. Several book features will help you not only to gain the confidence that you need to be convinced that you know some material already, but also to determine which topics you need to study more.

Organization of This Book

Although this book could be read cover-to-cover, we strongly advise against it. The book is designed to be a simple listing of those commands that you need to understand to pass the ROUTE exam. Very little theory is included in the *Portable Command Guides*; they are designed to list commands needed at this level of study.

This book follows the list of objectives for the CCNP ROUTE exam:

- **Chapter 1: "Network Design Requirements"**—This chapter shows the Cisco Hierarchical Model of Network Design; the Cisco Enterprise Composite Network Model; the Cisco Service-Oriented Network Architecture (SONA); a comparison of routing protocols; a chart outlining where protocols should be implemented; and the PPDIOO network lifecycle.

- **Chapter 2: "Implementing an EIGRP-based Solution"**—This chapter covers EIGRP, including the design, implementation, verification, and troubleshooting of this protocol.

- **Chapter 3: "Implementing a Scalable Multiarea Network OSPF-based Solution"**—This chapter deals with OSPF, including a review of configuring OSPF, both single area (as a review) and multiarea. Topics include the design, implementation, verification, and troubleshooting of the protocol.

- **Chapter 4: "Implementing an IPv4-based Redistribution Solution"**—This chapter shows how to manipulate routing information. Topics include prefix lists, distribution lists, route maps, route redistribution, administrative distances, and static routes.

- **Chapter 5: "Implementing Path Control"**—This chapter deals with those tools and commands that can be used to help evaluate network performance issues and control the path. Topics include offset lists, Cisco IOS IP Service Level Agreements (SLAs), and policy-based routing using route maps.

- **Chapter 6: "Enterprise to ISP Connectivity"**—This chapter deals with the use of BGP to connect an enterprise network to a service provider. Topics include the configuration, verification, and troubleshooting of a BGP-based solution; BGP attributes; regular expressions; and BGP route filtering using access lists.

- **Chapter 7: "Implementing IPv6"**—This chapter provides information and commands regarding the implementation of IPv6. Topics include assigning IPv6 addresses; CEF and dCEF for IPv6; RIPng; OSPFv3; IPv6 and EIGRP; route redistribution; IPv6 transition techniques; NAT-PC for IPv6; static routes; and verifying and troubleshooting IPv6.

- **Chapter 8: "Routing for Branch Offices and Mobile Workers"**—This chapter deals with the connection, verification, and troubleshooting of remote locations within your network. Topics include verifying existing services; configuring DSL; configuring PPPoA; configuring a cable modem connection; connecting a teleworker to a branch office VPN; configuring IPsec site-to-site VPNs; and configuring GRE tunnels over IPsec.

Did We Miss Anything?

As educators, we are always interested to hear how our students, and now readers of our books, do on both vendor exams and future studies. If you would like to contact either of us and let us know how this book helped you in your certification goals, please do so. Did we miss anything? Let us know. Contact us at ccnpguide@empson.ca or through the Cisco Press website, www.ciscopress.com.

CHAPTER 1

Network Design Requirements

This chapter provides information concerning the following network design requirement topics:

- Cisco Hierarchical Model of Network Design
- Cisco Enterprise Composite Network Model
- Cisco Service-Oriented Network Architecture (SONA)
- Routing protocol comparison
- Where to implement protocols
- The Prepare, Plan, Design, Implement, Operate, and Optimize (PPDIOO) network lifecycle

No commands are associated with this module of the CCNP ROUTE course objectives.

Cisco Hierarchical Model of Network Design

Figure 1-1 shows the Cisco Hierarchical Network Model.

Figure 1-1   Cisco Hierarchical Network Model

Core
High-Speed Switching

Distribution
Policy-Based Connectivity

Access
Local and Remote Workgroup Access

Cisco Enterprise Composite Network Model

Figure 1-2 shows the Cisco Enterprise Composite Network Model.

Figure 1-2   Cisco Enterprise Composite Network Model

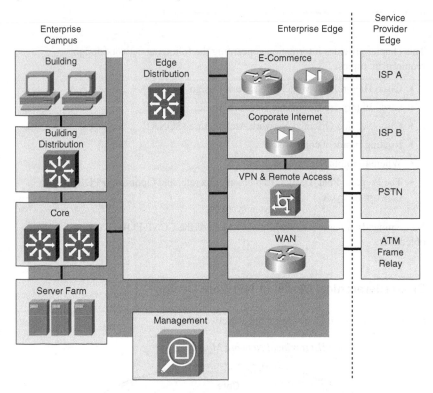

Cisco Service-Oriented Network Architecture

Figure 1-3 shows the Cisco Service-Oriented Network Architecture (SONA) framework.

Figure 1-3   Cisco SONA Framework

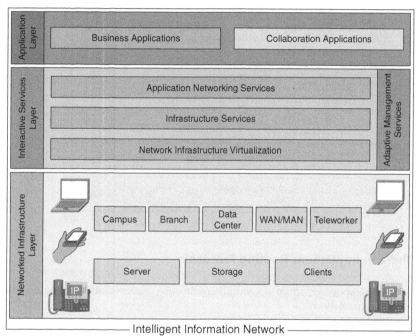

Routing Protocol Comparison

Figure 1-4 shows a comparison of EIGRP, OSPF, and BGP.

Figure 1-4   Comparing EIGRP, OSPF, and BGP (Figure Copyrighted by Cisco)

Parameters	EIGRP	OSPF	BGP
Size of Network (Small-Medium-Large-Very Large)	Large	Large	Very Large
Speed of Convergence (Very High-High-Medium-Low)	Very High	High	Slow
Use of VLSM (Yes-No)	Yes	Yes	Yes
Mixed-Vendor Devices (Yes-No)	No	Yes	Yes
Network Support Staff Knowledge (Good-Fair-Poor)	Good	Good	Fair

Where to Implement Routing Protocols

Figure 1-5 shows a comparison of where different routing protocols should be implemented in an enterprise network.

Figure 1-5   Routing Protocols (Figure Copyrighted by Cisco)

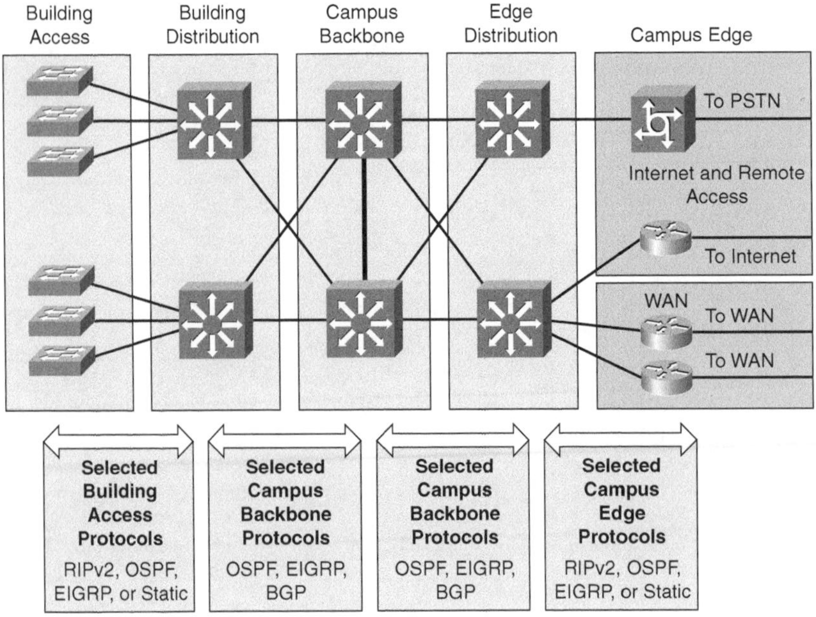

The Prepare, Plan, Design, Implement, Operate, and Optimize (PPDIOO) Network Lifecycle

Figure 1-6 shows the Prepare, Plan, Design, Implement, Operate, and Optimize (PPDIOO) lifecycle.

Figure 1-6   *Prepare, Plan, Design, Implement, Operate, and Optimize (PPDIOO) Network Lifecycle (Figure Copyrighted by Cisco)*

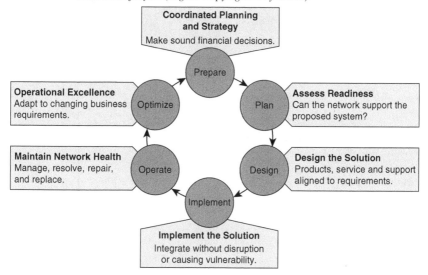

CHAPTER 2

Implementing an EIGRP-based Solution

This chapter provides information and commands concerning the following Enhanced Interior Gateway Routing Protocol (EIGRP) topics:

- Configuring EIGRP
- EIGRP auto-summarization
- Passive EIGRP interfaces
- "Pseudo" passive EIGRP interfaces
- Injecting a default route into EIGRP: redistribution of a static route
- Injecting a default route into EIGRP: IP default network
- Injecting a default route into EIGRP: summarize to 0.0.0.0/0
- Accepting exterior routing information: default-information
- Load balancing: maximum paths
- Load balancing: variance
- Bandwidth use
- Authentication
- Stub networks
- EIGRP unicast neighbors
- EIGRP over Frame Relay: dynamic mappings
- EIGRP over Frame Relay: static mappings
- EIGRP over Frame Relay: EIGRP over multipoint subinterfaces
- EIGRP over Frame Relay: EIGRP over point-to-point subinterfaces
- EIGRP over MPLS: Layer 2 VPN
- EIGRP over MPLS: Layer 3 VPN
- Verifying EIGRP
- Troubleshooting EIGRP
- Configuration example: EIGRP

Configuring EIGRP

`Router(config)#router eigrp 100`	Turns on the EIGRP process. 100 is the autonomous system number, which can be a number between 1 and 65,535. All routers in the same autonomous system must use the same autonomous system number.
`Router(config-router)#network 10.0.0.0`	Specifies which network to advertise in EIGRP.
`Router(config-router)#network 10.0.0.0 0.255.255.255`	Identifies which interfaces or networks to include in EIGRP. Interfaces must be configured with addresses that fall within the wildcard mask range of the **network** statement. A network mask can also be used here.
	NOTE: The use of a wildcard mask or network mask is optional.
	NOTE: There is no limit to the number of network statements (that is, **network** commands) that you can configure on a router.

TIP: If you are using the **network 172.16.1.0 0.0.0.255** command with a wildcard mask, in this example the command specifies that only interfaces on the 172.16.1.0/24 subnet will participate in EIGRP. However, because EIGRP automatically summarizes routes on the major network boundary by default, the full Class B network of 172.16.0.0 will be advertised. This occurs on advertisements out interfaces that have an IP address of a different major network address.

NOTE: If you do not use the optional wildcard mask, the EIGRP process assumes that all directly connected networks that are part of the overall major network will participate in the EIGRP process and EIGRP will attempt to establish neighbor relationships from each interface that is part of that Class A, B, or C major network.

Router(config-router)#eigrp log-neighbor-changes	Displays changes with neighbors.
Router(config-if)#bandwidth x	Sets the bandwidth of this interface to x kilobits to allow EIGRP to make a better metric calculation.
	TIP: The bandwidth command is used for metric calculations only. It does not change interface performance.
Router(config-router)#no network 10.0.0.0	Removes the network from the EIGRP process.
Router(config)#no router eigrp 100	Disables routing process 100.
Router(config-router)#metric weights tos k1 k2 k3 k4 k5	Changes the default k values used in metric calculation. These are the default values: tos=0, k1=1, k2=0, k3=1, k4=0, k5=0

NOTE: tos is a reference to the original IGRP intention to have IGRP perform type of service routing. Because this was never adopted into practice, the tos field in this command is always set to zero.

NOTE: With default settings in place, the metric of EIGRP is reduced to the slowest bandwidth plus the sum of all the delays of the exit interfaces from the local router to the destination network.

TIP: For two routers to form a neighbor relationship in EIGRP, the k values must match.

CAUTION: Unless you are very familiar with what is occurring in your network, it is recommended that you do not change the k values.

EIGRP Auto-Summarization

Router(config-router)#**auto-summary**	Enables auto-summarization for the EIGRP process.
Router(config-router)#**no auto-summary**	Turns off the auto-summarization feature.
Router(config)#**interface fastethernet 0/0**	Enters interface configuration mode.
Router(config-if)#**ip summary-address eigrp 100 10.10.0.0 255.255.0.0 75**	Enables manual summarization for EIGRP autonomous system 100 on this specific interface for the given address and mask. An administrative distance of 75 is assigned to this summary route.
	NOTE: The *administrative-distance* argument is optional in this command. Without it, an administrative distance of 5 is automatically applied to the summary route.

CAUTION: EIGRP automatically summarizes networks at the classful boundary. A poorly designed network with discontiguous subnets could have problems with connectivity if the summarization feature is left on. For instance, you could have two routers advertise the same network—172.16.0.0/16—when in fact they wanted to advertise two different networks—172.16.10.0/24 and 172.16.20.0/24.

Recommended practice is that you turn off automatic summarization if necessary, use the **ip summary-address** command, and summarize manually what you need to. A summary route will have the metric of the subnet with the lowest metric.

Passive EIGRP Interfaces

Router(config)#**router eigrp 110**	Starts the EIGRP routing process.
Router(config-router)#**network 10.0.0.0**	Specifies a network to advertise in the EIGRP routing process.
Router(config-router)#**passive-interface fastethernet 0/0**	Prevents the sending of Hello packets out the FastEthernet 0/0 interface. No neighbor adjacency will be formed.

Router(config-router)#**passive-interface default**	Prevents the sending of Hello packets out all interfaces.
Router(config)#**no passive-interface serial 0/0/1**	Enables Hello packets to be sent out interface serial 0/0/1, thereby allowing neighbor adjacencies to form.

"Pseudo" Passive EIGRP Interfaces

NOTE: A passive interface *cannot* send EIGRP Hellos, which prevents adjacency relationships with link partners.

An administrator can create a "pseudo" passive EIGRP interface by using a **route filter** that suppresses *all* routes from the EIGRP routing update. A neighbor relationship will form, but no routes will be sent out a specific interface.

Router(config)#**router eigrp 110**	Starts the EIGRP routing process.
Router(config-router)#**network 10.0.0.0**	Specifies a network to advertise in the EIGRP routing process.
Router(config-router)#**distribute-list 5 out serial 0/0/0**	Creates an outgoing distribute list for interface serial 0/0/0 and refers to ACL 5.
Router(config-router)#**exit**	Returns to global configuration mode.
Router(config)#**access-list 5 deny any**	Read this line to say, "All routing packets will be denied and not processed based on the parameters of distribute list 5."

Injecting a Default Route into EIGRP: Redistribution of a Static Route

Router(config)#**ip route 0.0.0.0 0.0.0.0 serial 0/0/0**	Creates a static default route to send all traffic with a destination network not in the routing table out interface serial 0/0/0.

	NOTE: Adding a static route to an Ethernet or other broadcast interface (for example, **ip route 0.0.0.0 0.0.0.0 fastethernet 1/2**) will cause the route to be inserted into the routing table only when the interface is up. This configuration is not generally recommended.
`Router(config)#`**`router eigrp 100`**	Creates EIGRP routing process 100.
`Router(config-router)#`**`redistribute static`**	Static routes on this router will be exchanged with neighbor routers in EIGRP.

NOTE: Use this method when you want to draw all traffic to unknown destinations to a default route at the core of the network.

NOTE: This method is effective for advertising connections to the Internet, but it will redistribute all static routes into EIGRP.

Injecting a Default Route into EIGRP: IP Default Network

`Router(config)#`**`router eigrp 100`**	Creates EIGRP routing process 100.
`Router(config-router)#`**`network 192.168.100.0`**	Specifies which network to advertise in EIGRP.
`Router(config-router)#`**`exit`**	Returns to global configuration mode.
`Router(config)#`**`ip route 0.0.0.0 0.0.0.0 192.168.100.5`**	Creates a static default route to send all traffic with a destination network not in the routing table to next-hop address 192.168.100.5.
`Router(config)#`**`ip default-network 192.168.100.0`**	Defines a route to the 192.168.100.0 network as a candidate default route.

NOTE: For EIGRP to propagate the route, the network specified by the **ip default-network** command must be known to EIGRP. This means the network must be an EIGRP-derived network in the routing table, or the static route used to generate the route to the network must be redistributed into EIGRP, or advertised into these protocols using the **network** command.

TIP: In a complex topology, many networks can be identified as candidate defaults. Without any dynamic protocols running, you can configure your router to choose from a number of candidate default routes based on whether the routing table has routes to networks other than 0.0.0.0/0. The **ip default-network** command enables you to configure robustness into the selection of a gateway of last resort. Rather than configuring static routes to specific next hops, you can have the router choose a default route to a particular network by checking in the routing table.

TIP: You can propagate the 0.0.0.0 network through EIGRP by using the network 0.0.0.0 statement.

Injecting a Default Route into EIGRP: Summarize to 0.0.0.0/0

`Router(config)#router eigrp 100`	Creates EIGRP routing process 100.
`Router(config-router)#network 192.168.100.0`	Specifies which network to advertise in EIGRP.
`Router(config-router)#exit`	Returns to global configuration mode.
`Router(config)#interface serial 0/0/0`	Enters interface configuration mode.
`Router(config-if)#ip address 192.168.100.1 255.255.255.0`	Assigns the IP address and subnet mask to the interface.
`Router(config-if)#ip summary-address eigrp 100 0.0.0.0 0.0.0.0 75`	Enables manual summarization for EIGRP autonomous system 100 on this specific interface for the given address and mask. An optional administrative distance of 75 is assigned to this summary route.

NOTE: Summarizing to a default route is effective only when you want to provide remote sites with a default route, and not propagate the default route toward the core of your network.

NOTE: Because summaries are configured per interface, you don't need to worry about using distribute lists or other mechanisms to prevent the default route from being propagated toward the core of your network.

Accepting Exterior Routing Information: default-information

Router(config)#**router eigrp 100**	Creates routing process 100.
Router(config-router)#**default-information in**	Allows exterior or default routes to be received by the EIGRP process autonomous system 100.
Router(config-router)#**no default-information in**	Suppresses exterior or default routing information.

Load Balancing: Maximum Paths

Router(config)#**router eigrp 100**	Creates routing process 100.
Router(config-router)#**network 10.0.0.0**	Specifies which network to advertise in EIGRP.
Router(config-router)#**maximum-paths 3**	Sets the maximum number of parallel routes that EIGRP will support to three.

NOTE: Up to 16 entries can be in the routing table for the same destination. The default is four.

NOTE: Setting the maximum-path to 1 disables load balancing.

Load Balancing: Variance

Router(config)#**router eigrp 100**	Creates routing process 100.
Router(config-router)#**network 10.0.0.0**	Specifies which network to advertise in EIGRP.
Router(config-router)#**variance** *n*	Instructs the router to include routes with a metric less than or equal to *n* times the minimum metric route for that destination, where *n* is the number specified by the **variance** command.

NOTE: If a path isn't a feasible successor, it isn't used in load balancing.

NOTE: EIGRP supports up to six unequal-cost paths.

NOTE: To control how traffic is distributed among routes when there are multiple routes for the same destination network that have different costs, use the **traffic-share balanced** command. Traffic is distributed proportionally to the ratio of the costs.

Bandwidth Use

Router(config)#**interface serial 0/0/0**	Enters interface configuration mode.
Router(config-if)#**bandwidth 256**	Sets the bandwidth of this interface to 256 kilobits to allow EIGRP to make a better metric calculation.
Router(config-if)#**ip bandwidth-percent eigrp 50 100**	Configures the percentage of bandwidth that may be used by EIGRP on an interface. 50 is the EIGRP autonomous system number. 100 is the percentage value. 100% * 256 = 256 kbps.

NOTE: By default, EIGRP is set to use only up to 50 percent of the bandwidth of an interface to exchange routing information. Values greater than 100 percent can be configured. This configuration option might prove useful if the bandwidth is set artificially low for other reasons, such as manipulation of the routing metric or to accommodate an oversubscribed multipoint Frame Relay configuration.

NOTE: The **ip bandwidth-percent** command relies on the value set by the **bandwidth** command.

Authentication

`Router(config)#interface serial 0/0/0`	Enters interface configuration mode.
`Router(config-if)#ip authentication mode eigrp 100 md5`	Enables Message Digest 5 (MD5) authentication in EIGRP packets over the interface.
`Router(config-if)#ip authentication key-chain eigrp 100 romeo`	Enables authentication of EIGRP packets. **romeo** is the name of the key chain.
`Router(config-if)#exit`	Returns to global configuration mode.
`Router(config)#key chain romeo`	Identifies a key chain. The name must match the name configured in interface configuration mode above.
`Router(config-keychain)#key 1`	Identifies the key number.
	NOTE: The range of keys is from 0 to 2147483647. The key identification numbers do not need to be consecutive. There must be at least one key defined on a key chain.
`Router(config-keychain-key)#key-string shakespeare`	Identifies the key string.
	NOTE: The string can contain from 1 to 80 upper- and lowercase alphanumeric characters, except that the first character cannot be a number.
`Router(config-keychain-key)#accept-lifetime start-time {infinite I end-time I duration seconds}`	Optionally specifies the period during which the key can be received.

	NOTE: The default start time and the earliest acceptable date is January 1, 1993. The default end time is an infinite time period.
`Router(config-keychain-key)#`**`send-lifetime`** `start-time` {**`infinite`** I `end-time` I **`duration`** `seconds`}	Optionally specifies the period during which the key can be sent.
	NOTE: The default start time and the earliest acceptable date is January 1, 1993. The default end time is an infinite period.

NOTE: For the start time and the end time to have relevance, ensure that the router knows the correct time. Recommended practice dictates that you run Network Time Protocol (NTP) or some other time-synchronization method if you intend to set lifetimes on keys.

Stub Networks

`Router(config)#`**`router eigrp 100`**	Creates routing process 100.
`Router(config-router)#`**`eigrp stub`**	Prompts the router to send updates containing its connected and summary routes only.
	NOTE: Only the stub router needs to have the **eigrp stub** command enabled.
`Router(config-router)#`**`eigrp stub connected`**	Permits the EIGRP stub routing feature to send only connected routes.
	NOTE: If the connected routes are not covered by a **network** statement, it might be necessary to redistribute connected routes with the **redistribute connected** command.
	TIP: The **connected** option is enabled by default.
`Router(config-router)#`**`eigrp stub static`**	Permits the EIGRP stub routing feature to send static routes.

	NOTE: Without this option, EIGRP will not send static routes, including internal static routes that normally would be automatically redistributed. It will still be necessary to redistribute static routes with the **redistribute static** command.
`Router(config-router)#eigrp` `stub summary`	Permits the EIGRP stub routing feature to send summary routes.
	NOTE: Summary routes can be created manually, or through automatic summarization at a major network boundary if the **auto-summary** command is enabled.
	TIP: The **summary** option is enabled by default.
`Router(config-router)#eigrp` `stub receive-only`	Restricts the router from sharing any of its routes with any other router in that EIGRP autonomous system.

NOTE: You can use the three optional arguments (**connected, static**, and **summary**) as part of the same command on a single line:

`Router(config-router)#eigrp stub connected static summary`

You cannot use the keyword **receive-only** with any other option because it prevents any type of route from being sent.

TIP: If you use any of the three keywords (**connected, static, summary**) individually with the **eigrp stub** command, connected and summary routes will not be sent automatically. For example, if you use the command that follows, summary routes will not be permitted:

`Router(config-router)#eigrp stub connected static`

EIGRP Unicast Neighbors

R2(config)#**router eigrp 100**	Enables EIGRP routing for autonomous system 100.
R2(config-router)#**network 172.17.2.0 0.0.0.255**	Identifies which interfaces or networks to include in EIGRP. Interfaces must be configured with addresses that fall within the wildcard mask range of the network statement. A network mask can also be used here.
R2(config-router)#**network 192.168.1.0**	Identifies which networks to include in EIGRP.
R2(config-router)#**neighbor 192.168.1.101**	Identifies a specific neighbor with which to exchange routing information. Instead of using multicast packets to exchange information, unicast packets will now be used.

EIGRP over Frame Relay: Dynamic Mappings

Figure 2-1 shows the network topology for the configuration that follows, which shows how to configure EIGRP over Frame Relay using dynamic mappings.

Figure 2-1   Network Topology for EIGRP over Frame Relay Using Dynamic Mappings

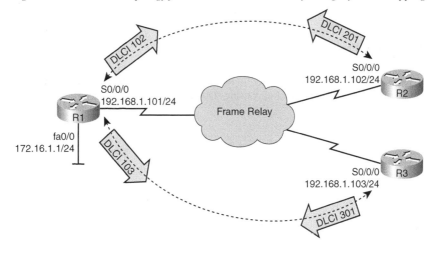

`R1(config)#interface serial 0/0/0`	Enters interface configuration mode.
`R1(config-if)#ip address 192.168.1.101 255.255.255.0`	Assigns the IP address and mask.
`R1(config-if)#encapsulation frame-relay`	Enables Frame Relay on this interface.
`R1(config-if)#no shutdown`	Enables the interface.
`R1(config-if)#exit`	Returns to global configuration mode.
`R1(config)#router eigrp 100`	Creates routing process 100.
`R1(config-router)#network 172.16.1.0 0.0.0.255`	Advertises the network in EIGRP.
`R1(config-router)#network 192.168.1.0`	Advertises the network in EIGRP.

NOTE: To deploy EIGRP over a physical interface using dynamic mappings—relying on Inverse ARP—no changes are needed to the basic EIGRP configuration.

NOTE: In EIGRP, split horizon is disabled by default on the physical interface. Therefore, R2 and R3 can provide connectivity between their connected networks. Inverse ARP does not provide dynamic mappings for communication between R2 and R3; this must be configured manually.

EIGRP over Frame Relay: Static Mappings

Figure 2-2 shows the network topology for the configuration that follows, which shows how to configure EIGRP over Frame Relay using static mappings.

Figure 2-2   Network Topology for EIGRP over Frame Relay Using Static Mappings

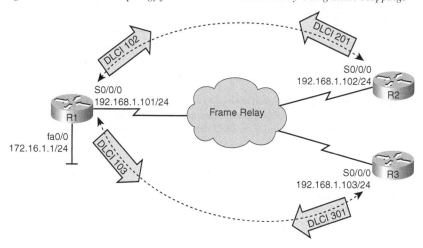

R1(config)#**interface serial 0/0/0**	Enters interface configuration mode.
R1(config-if)#**ip address 192.168.1.101 255.255.255.0**	Assigns the IP address and mask.
R1(config-if)#**encapsulation frame-relay**	Enables Frame Relay on this interface.
R1(config-if)#**frame-relay map ip 192.168.1.101 101**	Maps the IP address of 192.168.1.101 to DLCI 101.
	NOTE: The router includes this map to its own IP address so that the router can ping the local address from itself.
R1(config-if)#**frame-relay map ip 192.168.1.102 102 broadcast**	Maps the remote IP address 192.168.1.102 to DLCI 102. The **broadcast** keyword means that broadcasts will now be forwarded as well.
R1(config-if)#**frame-relay map ip 192.168.1.103 103 broadcast**	Maps the remote IP address 192.168.1.103 to DLCI 103. The **broadcast** keyword means that broadcasts will now be forwarded as well.
R1(config-if)#**no shutdown**	Enables the interface.
R1(config-if)#**exit**	Returns to global configuration mode.
R1(config)#**router eigrp 100**	Creates routing process 100.

R1(config-router)#**network** 172.16.1.0 0.0.0.255	Advertises the network in EIGRP.
R1(config-router)#**network** 192.168.1.0	Advertises the network in EIGRP.

NOTE: To deploy EIGRP over a physical interface using static mappings—and thus disabling Inverse ARP—no changes are needed to the basic EIGRP configuration. Only manual IP to DLCI mapping statements are required on all three routers.

NOTE: In EIGRP, split horizon is disabled by default on the physical interface. Therefore, R2 and R3 can provide connectivity between their connected networks. Inverse ARP does not provide dynamic mappings for communication between R2 and R3; this must be configured manually.

EIGRP over Frame Relay: EIGRP over Multipoint Subinterfaces

Figure 2-3 shows the network topology for the configuration that follows, which shows how to configure EIGRP over Frame Relay using multipoint subinterfaces.

Figure 2-3   *Network Topology for EIGRP over Frame Relay Using Multipoint Subinterfaces*

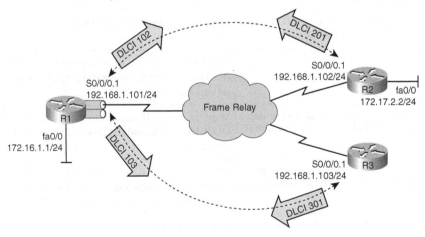

`R1(config)#interface serial 0/0/0`	Enters interface configuration mode.
`R1(config-if)#no ip address`	Removes any previous IP address and mask information assigned to this interface. Address now has no address or mask.
`R1(config-if)#encapsulation frame-relay`	Enables Frame Relay on this interface.
`R1(config-if)#no frame-relay inverse-arp eigrp 100`	Turns off dynamic mapping for EIGRP 100.
`R1(config-if)#exit`	Returns to global configuration mode.
`R1(config)#interface serial 0/0/0.1 multipoint`	Enables subinterface configuration mode. Multipoint behavior is also enabled.
`R1(config-subif)#ip address 192.168.1.101 255.255.255.0`	Assigns IP address and mask information.
`R1(config-subif)#no ip split-horizon eigrp 100`	Disables split horizon for EIGRP on this interface. This is to allow R2 and R3 to have connectivity between their connected networks.
`R1(config-subif)#frame-relay map ip 192.168.1.101 101`	Maps the IP address of 192.168.1.101 to DLCI 101.
	NOTE: The router includes this map to its own IP address so that the router can ping the local address from itself.
`R1(config-subif)#frame-relay map ip 192.168.1.102 102 broadcast`	Maps the remote IP address 192.168.1.102 to DLCI 102. The **broadcast** keyword means that broadcasts will now be forwarded as well.
`R1(config-subif)#frame-relay map ip 192.168.1.103 103 broadcast`	Maps the remote IP address 192.168.1.103 to DLCI 103. The **broadcast** keyword means that broadcasts will now be forwarded as well.
`R1(config-subif)#exit`	Returns to global configuration mode.
`R1(config)#router eigrp 100`	Creates routing process 100.
`R1(config-router)#network 172.16.1.0 0.0.0.255`	Advertises the network in EIGRP.
`R1(config-router)#network 192.168.1.0`	Advertises the network in EIGRP.

NOTE: To deploy EIGRP over multipoint subinterfaces, no changes are needed to the basic EIGRP configuration.

EIGRP over Frame Relay: EIGRP over Point-to-Point Subinterfaces

Figure 2-4 shows the network topology for the configuration that follows, which shows how to configure EIGRP over Frame Relay using point-to-point subinterfaces.

Figure 2-4   Network Topology for EIGRP over Frame Relay Using Point-to-Point Subinterfaces

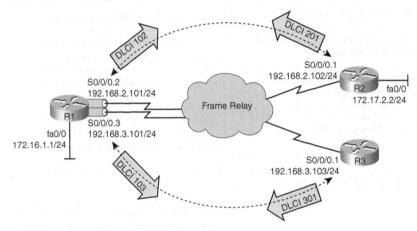

R1 Router

R1(config)#**interface serial 0/0/0**	Enters interface configuration mode.
R1(config-if)#**no ip address**	Removes any previous IP address and mask information assigned to this interface. Address now has no address or mask.
R1(config-if)#**encapsulation frame-relay**	Enables Frame Relay on this interface.
R1(config-if)#**exit**	Returns to global configuration mode.
R1(config)#**interface serial 0/0/0.2 point-to-point**	Enables subinterface configuration mode. Point-to-point behavior is also enabled.
R1(config-subif)#**ip address 192.168.2.101 255.255.255.0**	Assigns an IP address and mask to the subinterface.

`R1(config-subif)#`**`frame-relay`** **`interface-dlci 102`**	Assigns a local DLCI to this interface.
`R1(config-subif)#`**`exit`**	Returns to global configuration mode.
`R1(config)#`**`interface serial`** **`0/0/0.3 point-to-point`**	Enables subinterface configuration mode. Also enables point-to-point behavior.
`R1(config-subif)#`**`ip address`** **`192.168.3.101 255.255.255.0`**	Assigns an IP address and mask to the subinterface.
`R1(config-subif)#`**`frame-relay`** **`interface-dlci 103`**	Assigns a local DLCI to this interface.
`R1(config-subif)#`**`exit`**	Returns to global configuration mode.
`R1(config)#`**`router eigrp 100`**	Creates routing process 100.
`R1(config-router)#`**`network`** **`172.16.1.0 0.0.0.255`**	Advertises the network in EIGRP.
`R1(config-router)#`**`network`** **`192.168.2.0`**	Advertises the network in EIGRP.
`R1(config-router)#`**`network`** **`192.168.3.0`**	Advertises the network in EIGRP.

R3 Router

`R3(config)#`**`interface serial`** **`0/0/0`**	Enters interface configuration mode.
`R3(config-if)#`**`no ip address`**	Removes any previous IP address and mask information assigned to this interface. Address now has no address or mask.
`R3(config-if)#`**`encapsulation`** **`frame-relay`**	Enables Frame Relay on this interface.
`R3(config-if)#`**`exit`**	Returns to global configuration mode.
`R3(config)#`**`interface serial`** **`0/0/0.1 point-to-point`**	Enables subinterface configuration mode. Also enables point-to-point behavior.
`R3(config-subif)#`**`ip address`** **`192.168.3.103 255.255.255.0`**	Assigns an IP address and mask to the subinterface.
`R3(config-subif)#`**`frame-relay`** **`interface-dlci 103`**	Assigns a local DLCI to this interface.

R3(config-subif)#**exit**	Returns to global configuration mode.
R3(config)#**router eigrp 100**	Creates routing process 100.
R3(config-router)#**network 172.16.3.0 0.0.0.255**	Advertises the network in EIGRP.
R3(config-router)#**network 192.168.3.0**	Advertises the network in EIGRP.

NOTE: To deploy EIGRP over point-to-point subinterfaces, no changes are needed to the basic EIGRP configuration.

EIGRP over MPLS: Layer 2 VPN

Figure 2-5 shows the network topology for the configuration that follows, which shows how to configure EIGRP over MPLS (EoMPLS).

Figure 2-5   Network Topology for EIGRP over MPLS Layer 2 VPN

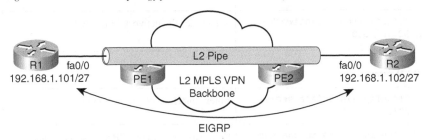

NOTE: In this example, it is assumed that the MPLS network is configured with transparent Layer 2 transport and only the EIGRP configuration is observed here.

R1 Router

R1(config)#**interface fastethernet 0/0**	Enters interface configuration mode.
R1(config-if)#**ip address 192.168.1.101 255.255.255.224**	Assigns the IP address and mask.
R1(config-if)#**no shutdown**	Enables the interface.

R1(config-if)#router eigrp 100	Creates routing process 100.
R1(config-router)#network 172.16.1.0 0.0.0.255	Advertises the network in EIGRP.
R1(config-router)#network 192.168.1.0	Advertises the network in EIGRP.

R2 Router

R2(config)#interface fastethernet 0/0	Enters interface configuration mode.
R2(config-if)#ip address 192.168.1.102 255.255.255.224	Assigns the IP address and mask.
R2(config-if)#no shutdown	Enables the interface.
R2(config-if)#router eigrp 100	Creates routing process 100.
R2(config-router)#network 172.17.2.0 0.0.0.255	Advertises the network in EIGRP.
R2(config-router)#network 192.168.1.0	Advertises the network in EIGRP.

NOTE: When deploying EIGRP over MPLS, no changes are needed to the basic EIGRP configuration from the customer perspective.

NOTE: From the EIGRP perspective, the MPLS backbone and routers PE1 and PE2 are not visible. A neighbor relationship is established directly between routers R1 and R2; this is verified with the **show ip eigrp neighbors** command output.

EIGRP over MPLS: Layer 3 VPN

Figure 2-6 shows the network topology for the configuration that follows, which shows how to configure EIGRP over MPLS where the MPLS PE devices are taking part in the EIGRP process.

Figure 2-6   *Network Topology for EIGRP over MPLS Layer 3 VPN*

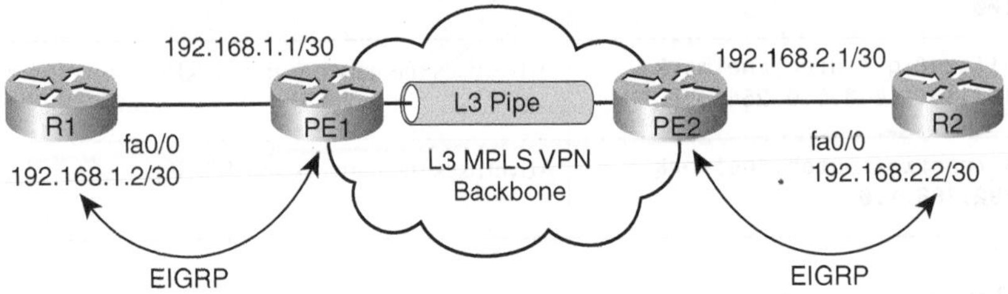

NOTE: In this example, it is assumed that the MPLS network is configured with the MPLS PE devices participating in the EIGRP process and virtual route forwarding. Only the client-side EIGRP configuration is observed here.

R1 Router

R1(config)#interface fastethernet 0/0	Enters interface configuration mode.
R1(config-if)#ip address 192.168.1.2 255.255.255.252	Assigns the IP address and mask.
R1(config-if)#no shutdown	Enables the interface.
R1(config-if)#router eigrp 100	Creates routing process 100.
R1(config-router)#network 172.16.1.0 0.0.0.255	Advertises the network in EIGRP.
R1(config-router)#network 192.168.1.0	Advertises the network in EIGRP.

R2 Router

R2(config)#interface fastethernet 0/0	Enters interface configuration mode.
R2(config-if)#ip address 192.168.2.2 255.255.255.252	Assigns the IP address and mask.
R2(config-if)#no shutdown	Enables the interface.
R2(config-if)#router eigrp 100	Creates routing process 100.

R2(config-router)#**network** 172.17.2.0 0.0.0.255	Advertises the network in EIGRP.
R2(config-router)#**network** 192.168.2.0	Advertises the network in EIGRP.

NOTE: When deploying EIGRP over Metro Ethernet, no changes are needed to the basic EIGRP configuration from the customer perspective. The only difference here is that the customer has to agree upon the EIGRP parameters—autonomous system numbers, authentication password, and so on—with the service provider, as these parameters are often governed by the service provider.

NOTE: The PE routers receive IPv4 routing updates from the CE routers and install them in the appropriate Virtual Routing and Forwarding (VRF) table. This part of the configuration and operation is the responsibility of the service provider.

NOTE: From the EIGRP perspective, the MPLS backbone and routers PE1 and PE2 are not visible. A neighbor relationship is established directly between routers R1 and R2; this is verified with the **show ip eigrp neighbors** command output.

Verifying EIGRP

Router#**show ip eigrp neighbors**	Displays the neighbor table.
Router#**show ip eigrp neighbors detail**	Displays a detailed neighbor table.
	TIP: The **show ip eigrp neighbors detail** command will verify whether a neighbor is configured as a stub router.
Router#**show ip eigrp interfaces**	Shows info for each interface.
Router#**show ip eigrp interface serial 0/0/0**	Shows info for specific interface.
Router#**show ip eigrp interface 100**	Shows info for interfaces running process 100.
Router#**show ip eigrp topology**	Displays the topology table.
	TIP: The **show ip eigrp topology** command shows you where your feasible successors are.

Router#**show ip eigrp traffic**	Shows the number and type of packets sent and received.
Router#**show ip protocols**	Shows the parameters and current state of the active routing protocol process.
Router#**show ip route**	Shows the complete routing table.
Router#**show ip route eigrp**	Shows a routing table with only EIGRP entries.
Router#**show key-chain**	Shows authentication key information.

Troubleshooting EIGRP

Router#**debug eigrp fsm**	Displays events/actions related to EIGRP feasible successor metrics (FSM).
Router#**debug eigrp packet**	Displays events/actions related to EIGRP packets.
Router#**debug eigrp neighbor**	Displays events/actions related to your EIGRP neighbors.
Router#**debug ip eigrp**	Displays events/actions related to EIGRP protocol packets.
Router#**debug ip eigrp notifications**	Displays EIGRP event notifications.

Configuration Example: EIGRP

Figure 2-7 shows the network topology for the configuration that follows, which shows how to configure EIGRP using commands covered in this chapter.

Figure 2-7   Network Topology for EIGRP Configuration

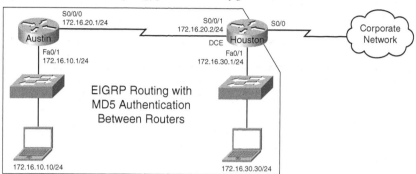

Austin Router

Austin>**enable**	Enters privileged mode.
Austin#**configure terminal**	Enters global configuration mode.
Austin(config)#**interface serial 0/0/0**	Enters interface configuration mode.
Austin(config-if)#**ip address 172.16.20.1 255.255.255.0**	Assigns the IP address and mask.
Austin(config-if)#**ip authentication mode eigrp 100 md5**	Enables MD5 authentication in EIGRP packets.
Austin(config-if)#**ip authentication key-chain eigrp 100 susannah**	Enables authentication of EIGRP packets. **susannah** is the name of the key chain.
Austin(config-if)#**no shutdown**	Enables the interface.
Austin(config-if)#**interface fastethernet 0/1**	Enters interface configuration mode.
Austin(config-if)#**ip address 172.16.10.1 255.255.255.0**	Assigns the IP address and mask.
Austin(config-if)#**no shutdown**	Enables the interface.
Austin(config-if)#**router eigrp 100**	Enables EIGRP routing.
Austin(config-router)#**no auto-summary**	Disables auto-summarization.
Austin(config-router)#**eigrp log-neighbor-changes**	Displays changes with neighbors.

`Austin(config-router)#network 172.16.0.0`	Advertises directly connected networks (classful address only).
`Austin(config-router)#eigrp stub`	Declares this router to be a stub router.
`Austin(config-router)#key chain susannah`	Identifies a key chain name, which must match the name configured in interface configuration mode.
`Austin(config-keychain)#key 1`	Identifies the key number.
`Austin(config-keychain-key)#key-string tower`	Identifies the key string.
`Austin(config-keychain-key)#accept-lifetime 06:30:00 Apr 19 2010 infinite`	Specifies the period during which the key can be received.
`Austin(config-keychain-key)#send-lifetime 06:30:00 Apr 19 2010 09:45:00 Apr 19 2010`	Specifies the period during which the key can be sent.
`Austin(config-keychain-key)#exit`	Returns to global configuration mode.
`Austin(config)#exit`	Returns to privileged mode.
`Austin#copy running-config startup-config`	Saves the configuration to NVRAM.

Houston Router

`Houston>enable`	Enters privileged mode.
`Houston#configure terminal`	Enters global configuration mode.
`Houston(config)#interface serial 0/0/1`	Enters interface configuration mode.
`Houston(config-if)#ip address 172.16.20.2 255.255.255.0`	Assigns the IP address and mask.
`Houston(config-if)#ip authentication mode eigrp 100 md5`	Enables MD5 authentication in EIGRP packets.
`Houston(config-if)#ip authentication key-chain eigrp 100 eddie`	Enables authentication of EIGRP packets. **eddie** is the name of the key chain.
`Houston(config-if)#clock rate 56000`	Sets the clock rate.
`Houston(config-if)#no shutdown`	Enables the interface.

`Houston(config-if)#`**`interface fastethernet 0/1`**	Enters interface configuration mode.
`Houston(config-if)#`**`ip address 172.16.30.1 255.255.255.0`**	Assigns the IP address and mask.
`Houston(config-if)#`**`no shutdown`**	Enables the interface.
`Houston(config-if)#`**`router eigrp 100`**	Enables EIGRP routing.
`Houston(config-router)#`**`no auto-summary`**	Disables auto-summarization.
`Houston(config-router)#`**`eigrp log-neighbor-changes`**	Displays changes with neighbors.
`Houston(config-router)#`**`network 172.16.0.0`**	Advertises directly connected networks (classful address only).
`Houston(config-router)#`**`key chain eddie`**	Identifies a key chain name, which must match the name configured in interface configuration mode.
`Houston(config-keychain)#`**`key 1`**	Identifies the key number.
`Houston(config-keychain-key)#`**`key-string tower`**	Identifies the key string.
`Houston(config-keychain-key)#`**`accept-lifetime 06:30:00 Apr 19 2010 infinite`**	Specifies the period during which the key can be received.
`Houston(config-keychain-key)#`**`send-lifetime 06:30:00 Apr 19 2010 09:45:00 Apr 19 2010`**	Specifies the period during which the key can be sent.
`Houston(config-keychain-key)#`**`exit`**	Returns to global configuration mode.
`Houston(config)#`**`exit`**	Returns to privileged mode.
`Houston#`**`copy run start`**	Saves the configuration to NVRAM.

CHAPTER 3

Implementing a Scalable Multiarea Network OSPF-based Solution

This chapter provides information and commands concerning the following Open Shortest Path First (OSPF) topics:

- Configuring OSPF
- Using wildcard masks with OSPF areas
- Configuring multiarea OSPF
- Loopback interfaces
- Router ID
- DR/BDR elections
- Passive interfaces
- Modifying cost metrics
- OSPF LSDB overload protection
- OSPF **auto-cost reference-bandwidth**
- Authentication: simple
- Authentication: using MD5 encryption
- Timers
- Propagating a default route
- OSPF special area types
  - Stub areas
  - Totally stubby areas
  - Not-so-stubby areas (NSSA) stub area
  - NSSA totally stubby areas
- Route summarization
  - Inter-area route summarization
  - External route summarization
- Configuration example: virtual links
- OSPF and NBMA networks
  - Full-mesh Frame Relay: NBMA on physical interfaces
  - Full-mesh Frame Relay: broadcast on physical interfaces
  - Full-mesh Frame Relay: point-to-multipoint networks
  - Full-mesh Frame Relay: point-to-point networks on subinterfaces
- OSPF over NBMA topology summary
- Verifying OSPF Configuration
- Troubleshooting OSPF

- Configuration example: single-area OSPF
- Configuration example: multiarea OSPF
- Configuration example: OSPF and NBMA networks
- Configuration example: OSPF and broadcast networks
- Configuration example: OSPF and point-to-multipoint networks
- Configuration example: OSPF and point-to-point networks using subinterfaces

Configuring OSPF

Router(config)#**router ospf 123**	Starts OSPF process 123. The process ID is any positive integer value between 1 and 65,535. The process ID is *not* related to the OSPF area. The process ID merely distinguishes one process from another within the device.
Router(config-router)#**network 172.16.10.0 0.0.0.255 area 0**	OSPF advertises interfaces, not networks. Uses the wildcard mask to determine which interfaces to advertise. Read this line to say, "Any interface with an address of 172.16.10.x is to be put into area 0."
	NOTE: The process ID number of one router does not have to match the process ID of any other router. Unlike Enhanced Interior Gateway Routing Protocol (EIGRP), matching this number across all routers does *not* ensure that network adjacencies will form.
Router(config-router)#**log-adjacency-changes detail**	Configures the router to send a syslog message when there is a change of state between OSPF neighbors.
	TIP: Although the **log-adjacency-changes** command is on by default, only up/down events are reported unless you use the **detail** keyword.

Using Wildcard Masks with OSPF Areas

When compared to an IP address, a wildcard mask will identify what addresses get matched for placement into an area:

- A 0 (zero) in a wildcard mask means to check the corresponding bit in the address for an exact match.
- A 1 (one) in a wildcard mask means to ignore the corresponding bit in the address—can be either 1 or 0.

Example 1: 172.16.0.0 0.0.255.255

$$
\begin{array}{rl}
172.16.0.0 = & 10101100.00010000.00000000.00000000 \\
0.0.255.255 = & 00000000.00000000.11111111.11111111 \\
\hline
result = & 10101100.00010000.xxxxxxxx.xxxxxxxx
\end{array}
$$

172.16.x.x (Anything between 172.16.0.0 and 172.16.255.255 will match the example statement.)

> **TIP:** An octet of all zeros means that the octet has to match the address exactly. An octet of all ones means that the octet can be ignored.

Example 2: 172.16.8.0 0.0.7.255

$$
\begin{array}{rl}
172.168.8.0 = & 10101100.00010000.00001000.00000000 \\
0.0.0.7.255 = & 00000000.00000000.00000111.11111111 \\
\hline
result = & 10101100.00010000.00001xxx.xxxxxxxx \\
00001xxx = & 00001000 \text{ to } 00001111 = 8 - 15 \\
xxxxxxxx = & 00000000 \text{ to } 11111111 = 0 - 255
\end{array}
$$

Anything between 172.16.8.0 and 172.16.15.255 will match the example statement.

`Router(config-router)#network` `172.16.10.1 0.0.0.0 area 0`	Read this line to say, "Any interface with an exact address of 172.16.10.1 is to be put into area 0."
`Router(config-router)#network` `172.16.10.0 0.0.255.255 area 0`	Read this line to say, "Any interface with an address of 172.16.x.x is to be put into area 0."
`Router(config-router)#network 0.0.0.0` `255.255.255.255 area 0`	Read this line to say, "Any interface with any address is to be put into area 0."

Configuring Multiarea OSPF

`Router(config)#router ospf 1`	Starts OSPF process 1.
`Router(config-router)#network 172.16.10.0 0.0.0.255 area 0`	Read this line to say, "Any interface with an address of 172.16.10.x is to be put into area 0."
`Router(config-router)#network 10.10.10.1 0.0.0.0 area 51`	Read this line to say, "Any interface with an exact address of 10.10.10.1 is to be put into area 51."

Loopback Interfaces

`Router(config)#interface loopback0`	Creates a virtual interface named Loopback 0 and then moves the router to interface configuration mode.
`Router(config-if)#ip address 192.168.100.1 255.255.255.255`	Assigns the IP address to the interface.
	NOTE: Loopback interfaces are always "up and up" and do not go down unless manually shut down. This makes loopback interfaces great for use as an OSPF router ID.

Router ID

`Router(config)#router ospf 1`	Starts OSPF process 1.
`Router(config-router)#router-id 10.1.1.1`	Sets the router ID to 10.1.1.1. If this command is used on an OSPF router process that is already active (has neighbors), the new router ID is used at the next reload or at a manual OSPF process restart.
`Router(config-router)#no router-id 10.1.1.1`	Removes the static router ID from the configuration. If this command is used on an OSPF router process that is already active (has neighbors), the old router ID behavior is used at the next reload or at a manual OSPF process restart.

DR/BDR Elections

`Router(config)#interface serial 0/0/0`	Enters interface configuration mode.
`Router(config-if)#ip ospf priority 50`	Changes the OSPF interface priority to 50.
	NOTE: The assigned priority can be between 0 and 255. A priority of 0 makes the router ineligible to become a designated router (DR) or backup designated router (BDR). The highest priority wins the election. A priority of 255 guarantees a tie in the election. If all routers have the same priority, regardless of the priority number, they tie. Ties are broken by the highest router ID.

Passive Interfaces

`Router(config)#router ospf 1`	Starts OSPF process 1.
`Router(config-router)#network 172.16.10.0 0.0.0.255 area 0`	Read this line to say "Any interface with an address of 172.16.10.x is to be put into area 0."
`Router(config-router)#passive-interface fastethernet 0/0`	Disables the sending of routing updates on this interface.
`Router(config-router)#passive-interface default`	Disables the sending of routing updates out all interfaces.
`Router(config-router)#no passive-interface serial 0/0/1`	Enables routing updates to be sent out interface serial 0/0/1, thereby allowing neighbor adjacencies to form.

Modifying Cost Metrics

Router(config)#**interface serial 0/0/0**	Enters interface configuration mode.
Router(config-if)#**bandwidth 128**	If you change the bandwidth, OSPF will recalculate the cost of the link.
Or	
Router(config-if)#**ip ospf cost 1564**	Changes the cost to a value of 1564.
	NOTE: The cost of a link is determined by dividing the reference bandwidth by the interface bandwidth. The bandwidth of the interface is a number between 1 and 10,000,000. The unit of measurement is kilobits. The cost is a number between 1 and 65,535. The cost has no unit of measurement; it is just a number.

OSPF LSDB Overload Protection

Router(config)#**router ospf 1**	Starts OSPF process 1.
Router(config-if)#**max-lsa 12000**	Limits the number of nonself-generated link-state advertisements (LSA).

NOTE: If other routers are configured incorrectly, causing, for example, a redistribution of a large number of prefixes, large numbers of LSAs can be generated. This can drain local CPU and memory resources. With the **max-lsa** *x* feature enabled, the router keeps count of the number of received (nonself-generated) LSAs that it keeps in its link-state database (LSDB). An error message is logged when this number reaches a configured threshold number, and a notification is sent when it exceeds the threshold number.

If the LSA count still exceeds the threshold after one minute, the OSPF process takes down all adjacencies and clears the OSPF database. This is called the *ignore state*. In the ignore state, no OSPF packets are sent or received by interfaces that belong to the OSPF process.

The OSPF process will remain in the ignore state for the time that is defined by the **ignore-time** parameter. If the OSPF process remains normal for the time that is defined by the **reset-time** parameter, the ignore state counter is reset to 0.

OSPF auto-cost reference-bandwidth

Router(config)#**router ospf 1**	Starts OSPF process 1.
Router(config-router)#**auto-cost reference-bandwidth 1000**	Changes the reference bandwidth that OSPF uses to calculate the cost of an interface.
	NOTE: The range of the reference bandwidth is 1 to 4,294,967. The default is 100. The unit of measurement is Mbps.
	NOTE: The value set by the **ip ospf cost** command overrides the cost resulting from the **auto-cost** command.
	TIP: If you use the command **auto-cost reference-bandwidth** *reference-bandwidth*, configure all the routers to use the same value. Failure to do so will result in routers using a different reference cost to calculate the shortest path, resulting in potential suboptimum routing paths.

Authentication: Simple

Router(config)#**router ospf 1**	Starts OSPF process 1.
Router(config-router)#**area 0 authentication**	Enables simple authentication; the password will be sent in clear text.
	NOTE: Another way to enable authentication is to move to the interface in which you want authentication to take place and enter the following command: Router(config-if)#**ip ospf authentication**
Router(config-router)#**exit**	Returns to global configuration mode.

Router(config)#**interface fastethernet 0/0**	Enters interface configuration mode.
Router(config-if)#**ip ospf authentication-key fred**	Sets key (password) to fred.
	NOTE: The password can be any continuous string of characters that can be entered from the keyboard, up to eight characters in length. To be able to exchange OSPF information, all neighboring routers on the same network must have the same password.
	NOTE: In Cisco IOS Release 12.4, the router will give a warning if you try to configure a password longer than eight characters; only the first eight characters will be used. Some earlier Cisco IOS releases did not provide this warning.

Authentication: Using MD5 Encryption

Router(config)#**router ospf 1**	Starts OSPF process 1.
Router(config-router)#**area 0 authentication message-digest**	Enables authentication with MD5 password encryption.
	NOTE: Another way to enable authentication is to move to the interface in which you want authentication to take place and enter the following command: Router(config-if)#**ip ospf authentication message-digest**
Router(config-router)#**exit**	Returns to global configuration mode.
Router(config)#**interface fastethernet 0/0**	Enters interface configuration mode.
Router(config-if)#**ip ospf message-digest-key 1 md5 fred**	1 is the *key-id*. This value must be the same as that of your neighboring router. **md5** indicates that the MD5 hash algorithm will be used. **fred** is the key (password) and must be the same as that of your neighboring router.

	NOTE: If the **service password-encryption** command is not used when implementing OSPF MD5 authentication, the MD5 secret will be stored as plain text in NVRAM.
	NOTE: In Cisco IOS Release 12.4, the router will give a warning if you try to configure a password longer than 16 characters; only the first 16 characters will be used. Some earlier Cisco IOS releases did not provide this warning.

TIP: It is recommended that you keep no more than one key per interface. Every time you add a new key, you should remove the old key to prevent the local system from continuing to communicate with a hostile system that knows the old key.

NOTE: If the **service password-encryption** command is not used when configuring OSPF authentication, the key will be stored as plain text in the router configuration. If you use the **service password-encryption** command, there will be an *encryption-type* of 7 specified before the encrypted key.

Timers

`Router(config-if)#`**`ip ospf hello-interval timer 20`**	Changes the Hello Interval timer to 20 seconds.
`Router(config-if)#`**`ip ospf dead-interval 80`**	Changes the Dead Interval timer to 80 seconds.
	NOTE: Hello and Dead Interval timers must match for routers to become neighbors.

NOTE: If you change the Hello Interval timer, the Dead Interval timer will automatically be adjusted to four times the new Hello Interval timer.

Propagating a Default Route

`Router(config)#ip route 0.0.0.0` `0.0.0.0 serial 0/0/0`	Creates a default route.
`Router(config)#router ospf 1`	Starts OSPF process 1.
`Router(config-router)#default-` `information originate`	Sets the default route to be propagated to all OSPF routers.
`Router(config-router)#default-` `information originate always`	The **always** option will propagate a default "quad-zero" route even if one is not configured on this router.
	NOTE: The **default-information originate** command or the **default-information originate always** command is usually only to be configured on your "entrance" or "gateway" router, the router that connects your network to the outside world—the Autonomous System Boundary Router (ASBR).

OSPF Special Area Types

This section covers four different special areas with respect to OSPF:

- Stub areas
- Totally stubby areas
- Not-so-stubby areas (NSSA) stub area
- NSSA totally stubby areas

Stub Areas

`ABR(config)#router ospf 1`	Starts OSPF process 1.
`ABR(config-router)#network 172.16.10.0` `0.0.0.255 area 0`	Read this line to say, "Any interface with an address of 172.16.10.x is to be put into area 0."
`ABR(config-router)#network 172.16.20.0` `0.0.0.255 area 51`	Read this line to say, "Any interface with an address of 172.16.20.x is to be put into area 51."

ABR(config-router)#**area 51 stub**	Defines area 51 as a stub area.
ABR(config-router)#**area 51 default-cost 10**	Defines the cost of a default route sent into the stub area. Default is 1.
	NOTE: This is an optional command.
Internal(config)#**router ospf 1**	Starts OSPF process 1.
Internal(config-router)#**network 172.16.20.0 0.0.0.255 area 51**	Read this line to say, "Any interface with an address of 172.16.20.*x* is to be put into area 51."
Internal(config-router)#**area 51 stub**	Defines area 51 as a stub area.
	NOTE: All routers in the stub area must be configured with the **area** *x* **stub** command, including the Area Border Router (ABR).

Totally Stubby Areas

ABR(config)#**router ospf 1**	Starts OSPF process 1.
ABR(config-router)#**network 172.16.10.0 0.0.0.255 area 0**	Read this line to say, "Any interface with an address of 172.16.10.*x* is to be put into area 0."
ABR(config-router)#**network 172.16.20.0 0.0.0.255 area 51**	Read this line to say, "Any interface with an address of 172.16.20.*x* is to be put into area 51."
ABR(config-router)#**area 51 stub no-summary**	Defines area 51 as a totally stubby area.
Internal(config)#**router ospf 1**	Starts OSPF process 1.
Internal(config-router)#**network 172.16.20.0 0.0.0.255 area 51**	Read this line to say, "Any interface with an address of 172.16.20.*x* is to be put into area 51."
Internal(config-router)#**area 51 stub**	Defines area 51 as a stub area.
	NOTE: Whereas all internal routers in the area are configured with the **area** *x* **stub** command, the ABR is configured with the **area** *x* **stub no-summary** command.

Not-So-Stubby Areas (NSSA) Stub Area

`ABR(config)#router ospf 1`	Starts OSPF process 1.
`ABR(config-router)#network 172.16.10.0 0.0.0.255 area 0`	Read this line to say, "Any interface with an address of 172.16.10.x is to be put into area 0."
`ABR(config-router)#network 172.16.20.0 0.0.0.255 area 1`	Read this line to say, "Any interface with an address of 172.16.20.x is to be put into area 1."
`ABR(config-router)#area 1 nssa`	Defines area 1 as an NSSA stub area.
`Internal(config)#router ospf 1`	Starts OSPF process 1.
`Internal(config-router)#network 172.16.20.0 0.0.0.255 area 1`	Read this line to say, "Any interface with an address of 172.16.20.x is to be put into area 1."
`Internal(config-router)#area 1 nssa`	Defines area 1 as an NSSA stub area.
	NOTE: All routers in the NSSA stub area must be configured with the **area** *x* **nssa** command.

NSSA Totally Stubby Areas

`ABR(config)#router ospf 1`	Starts OSPF process 1.
`ABR(config-router)#network 172.16.10.0 0.0.0.255 area 0`	Read this line to say, "Any interface with an address of 172.16.10.x is to be put into area 0."
`ABR(config-router)#network 172.16.20.0 0.0.0.255 area 11`	Read this line to say, "Any interface with an address of 172.16.20.x is to be put into area 11."
`ABR(config-router)#area 11 nssa no-summary`	Defines area 11 as an NSSA totally stubby area.
`Internal(config)#router ospf 1`	Starts OSPF process 1.
`Internal(config-router)#network 172.16.20.0 0.0.0.255 area 11`	Read this line to say, "Any interface with an address of 172.16.20.x is to be put into area 11."

`Internal(config-router)#`**`area 11 nssa`**	Defines area 11 as an NSSA stub area.
	NOTE: Whereas all internal routers in the area are configured with the **area** *x* **nssa** command, the ABR is configured with the **area** *x* **nssa no-summary** command.

Route Summarization

In OSPF, there are two different types of summarization:

- Inter-area route summarization
- External route summarization

The sections that follow provide the commands necessary to configure both types of summarization.

Inter-Area Route Summarization

`Router(config)#`**`router ospf 1`**	Starts OSPF process 1.
`Router(config-router)#`**`area 1 range`** **`192.168.64.0 255.255.224.0`**	Configures the ABR to consolidate routes to this summary address before injecting them into a different area.
	NOTE: This command is to be configured on an ABR only.
	NOTE: By default, ABRs do *not* summarize routes between areas.

External Route Summarization

`Router(config)#`**`router ospf 123`**	Starts OSPF process 1.
`Router(config-router)#`**`summary-`** **`address 192.168.64.0 255.255.224.0`**	Advertises a single route for all the redistributed routes that are covered by a specified network address and netmask.

	NOTE: This command is to be configured on an ASBR only.
	NOTE: By default, ASBRs do *not* summarize routes.

Configuration Example: Virtual Links

Figure 3-1 shows the network topology for the configuration that follows, which demonstrates how to create a virtual link.

Figure 3-1   Virtual Areas: OSPF

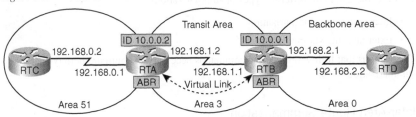

RTA(config)#**router ospf 1**	Starts OSPF process 1.
RTA(config-router)#**router-id 10.0.0.2**	Sets the router ID to 10.0.0.2.
RTA(config-router)#**network 192.168.0.0 0.0.0.255 area 51**	Read this line to say, "Any interface with an address of 192.168.0.*x* is to be put into area 51."
RTA(config-router)#**network 192.168.1.0 0.0.0.255 area 3**	Read this line to say, "Any interface with an address of 192.168.1.*x* is to be put into area 3."
RTA(config-router)#**area 3 virtual-link 10.0.0.1**	Creates a virtual link with RTB.
RTB(config)#**router ospf 1**	Starts OSPF process 1.
RTB(config-router)#**router-id 10.0.0.1**	Sets the router ID to 10.0.0.1.
RTB(config-router)#**network 192.168.1.0 0.0.0.255 area 3**	Read this line to say, "Any interface with an address of 192.168.1.*x* is to be put into area 3."
RTB(config-router)#**network 192.168.2.0 0.0.0.255 area 0**	Read this line to say, "Any interface with an address of 192.168.2.*x* is to be put into area 0."

RTB(config-router)#**area 3 virtual-link 10.0.0.2**	Creates a virtual link with RTA.
	NOTE: A virtual link has the following two requirements: It must be established between two routers that share a common area and are both ABRs. One of these two routers must be connected to the backbone.
	NOTE: A virtual link is a temporary solution to a topology problem.
	NOTE: A virtual link cannot be configured through stub areas.

OSPF and NBMA Networks

OSPF is not well suited for nonbroadcast multiaccess (NBMA) networks such as Frame Relay or ATM. The term *multiaccess* means that an NBMA cloud is seen as a single network that has multiple devices attached to it, much like an Ethernet network. However, the *nonbroadcast* part of NBMA means that a packet sent into this network might not be seen by all other routers, which differs from broadcast technologies such as Ethernet. OSPF will want to elect a DR and BDR because an NBMA network is multiaccess; however, because the network is also nonbroadcast, there is no guarantee that all OSPF packets, such as Hello packets, would be received by other routers. This could affect the election of the DR because not all routers would know about all the other routers. The following sections list some possible solutions to dealing with OSPF in NBMA networks.

Full-Mesh Frame Relay: NBMA on Physical Interfaces

Router(config)#**router ospf 1**	Starts OSPF process 1.
Router(config-router)#**network 10.1.1.0 0.0.0.255 area 0**	Read this line to say, "Any interface with an address of 10.1.1.*x* is to be put into area 0."
Router(config-router)#**neighbor 10.1.1.2**	Manually identifies this router's neighbor at IP address 10.1.1.2.

Router(config-router)#neighbor 10.1.1.3 priority 15	Manually identifies this router's neighbor at IP address 10.1.1.3 and assigns a priority value of 15 to determine the DR.
Router(config-router)#exit	Returns to global configuration mode.
Router(config)#interface serial 0/0/0	Moves to interface configuration mode.
Router(config-if)#encapsulation frame-relay	Enables Frame Relay on this interface.
Router(config-if)#ip address 10.1.1.1 255.255.255.0	Assigns an IP address and netmask to this interface.
Router(config-if)#ip ospf network non-broadcast	Defines OSPF nonbroadcast network type.
Router(config-if)#frame-relay map ip 10.1.1.2 100	Maps the remote IP address 10.1.1.2 to data-link connection identifier (DLCI) 100.
Router(config-if)#frame-relay map ip 10.1.1.3 200	Maps the remote IP address 10.1.1.3 to DLCI 200.
	NOTE: Using the **neighbor** command will allow for an OSPF router to exchange routing information without multicasts and instead use unicasts to the manually entered neighbor IP address.
	NOTE: Prior to Cisco IOS Release 12.0, the **neighbor** command applied to NBMA networks only. With Release 12.0, the **neighbor** command applies to NBMA networks and point-to-multipoint networks.

Full-Mesh Frame Relay: Broadcast on Physical Interfaces

Router(config)#interface serial 0/0/0	Moves to interface configuration mode.
Router(config-if)#encapsulation frame-relay	Enables Frame Relay on this interface.

`Router(config-if)#`**`ip address 10.1.1.1`** **`255.255.255.0`**	Assigns an IP address and netmask to this interface.
`Router(config-if)#`**`ip ospf network`** **`broadcast`**	Changes the network type from the default *NBMA* to *broadcast*.
`Router(config-if)#`**`ip ospf priority 15`**	Changes the OSPF interface priority to 15.
`Router(config-if)#`**`frame-relay map ip`** **`10.1.1.2 100 broadcast`**	Maps the remote IP address 10.1.1.2 to DLCI 100. Broadcast and multicast addresses will now be forwarded.
`Router(config-if)#`**`frame-relay map ip`** **`10.1.1.3 200 broadcast`**	Maps the remote IP address 10.1.1.3 to DLCI 200. Broadcast and multicast addresses will now be forwarded.
`Router(config-if)#`**`no shutdown`**	Enables the interface.
`Router(config)#`**`router ospf 1`**	Starts OSPF process 1.
`Router(config-router)#`**`network 10.1.1.0`** **`0.0.0.255 area 0`**	Read this line to say, "Any interface with an address of 10.1.1.x is to be put into area 0."
	NOTE: If you want to influence the DR election, another option is to create a fully meshed topology where every router has a permanent virtual circuit (PVC) to every other router. This is efficient in terms of NBMA network designs. However, this is also a costly solution. For n routers, you need $n(n-1)/2$ PVCs. A 5-router full mesh would mean 10 PVCs are needed; 20 routers would mean 190 PVCs are needed.

Full-Mesh Frame Relay: Point-to-Multipoint Networks

`Router(config)#interface serial 0/0/0`	Moves to interface configuration mode.
`Router(config-if)#encapsulation frame-relay`	Enables Frame Relay on this interface.
`Router(config-if)#ip address 10.1.1.1 255.255.255.0`	Assigns an IP address and netmask to this interface.
`Router(config-if)#ip ospf network point-to-multipoint`	Changes the network to a point-to-multipoint network.
`Router(config-if)#exit`	Returns to global configuration mode.
`Router(config)#router ospf 1`	Starts OSPF process 1.
`Router(config-router)#network 10.1.1.0 0.0.0.255 area 0`	Read this line to say, "Any interface with an address of 10.1.1.x is to be put into area 0."
	NOTE: In this example, Inverse ARP is used to dynamically map IP addresses to DLCIs. Static maps could have been used, if desired.
	NOTE: Point-to-multipoint networks treat PVCs as a collection of point-to-point links rather than a multiaccess network. No DR/BDR election will take place.
	NOTE: Point-to-multipoint networks might be your only alternative to broadcast networks in a multivendor environment.
`Router(config-router)#exit`	Returns to global configuration mode.
`Router(config)#interface serial 0/0/1`	Moves to interface configuration mode.
`Router(config)#ip ospf network point-to-multipoint non-broadcast`	Creates a point-to-multipoint nonbroadcast mode.

	NOTE: Point-to-multipoint nonbroadcast mode is a Cisco extension to the RFC-compliant point-to-multipoint mode. NOTE: Neighbors must be manually defined in this mode. NOTE: DR/BDRs are not used in this mode. NOTE: Point-to-multipoint nonbroadcast mode is used in special cases where neighbors cannot be automatically discovered.

NOTE: Point-to-multipoint networks can also be created on a subinterface with the following command:

```
Router(config)#interface serial 0/0/0.1 multipoint
```

NOTE: OSPF defaults to point-to-point mode on the point-to-point subinterface. OSPF defaults to nonbroadcast mode on the point-to-multipoint interface.

Full-Mesh Frame Relay: Point-to-Point Networks with Subinterfaces

`Router(config)#interface serial 0/0/0`	Moves to interface configuration mode.
`Router(config-if)#encapsulation frame-relay`	Enables Frame Relay on this interface.
`Router(config-if)#no shutdown`	Enables the interface.
`Router(config-if)#interface serial 0/0/0.300 point-to-point`	Creates subinterface 300 and makes it a point-to-point network.
`Router(config-subif)#ip address 192.168.1.1 255.255.255.252`	Assigns an IP address and netmask.
`Router(config-subif)#frame-relay interface-dlci 300`	Assigns DLCI 300 to the subinterface.
`Router(config-subif)#interface serial 0/0/0.400 point-to-point`	Creates subinterface 400 and makes it a point-to-point network.
`Router(config-subif)#ip address 192.168.1.5 255.255.255.252`	Assigns an IP address and netmask.

`Router(config-subif)#frame-relay interface-dlci 400`	Assigns DLCI 400 to the subinterface.
`Router(config-subif)#exit`	Returns to interface configuration mode.
`Router(config-if)#exit`	Returns to global configuration mode.
`Router(config)#router ospf 1`	Starts OSPF process 1.
`Router(config-router)#network 192.168.1.0 0.0.0.255 area 0`	Read this line to say, "Any interface with an address of 192.168.1.x is to be put into area 0."
	NOTE: Point-to-point subinterfaces allow each PVC to be configured as a separate subnet. No DR/BDR election will take place.
	NOTE: The use of subinterfaces increases the amount of memory used on the router.

OSPF over NBMA Topology Summary

OSPF Mode	NBMA Preferred Topology	Subnet Address	Hello Timer	Adjacency	RFC or Cisco
Broadcast	Full or partial mesh	Same	10 seconds	Automatic, DR/BDR elected	Cisco
Nonbroadcast (NBMA)	Full or partial mesh	Same	30 seconds	Manual configuration, DR/BDR elected	RFC
Point-to-multipoint	Partial mesh or star	Same	30 seconds	Automatic, no DR/BDR	RFC
Point-to-multipoint nonbroadcast	Partial mesh or star	Same	30 seconds	Manual Configuration, no DR/BDR	Cisco
Point-to-point	Partial mesh or star, using subinterface	Different for each Subinterface	10 seconds	Automatic, no DR/BDR	Cisco

Verifying OSPF Configuration

Router#**show ip protocol**	Displays parameters for all protocols running on the router.
Router#**show ip route**	Displays a complete IP routing table.
Router#**show ip ospf**	Displays basic information about OSPF routing processes.
Router#**show ip ospf border-routers**	Displays border and boundary router information.
Router#**show ip ospf database**	Displays the contents of the OSPF database.
Router#**show ip ospf database nssa-external**	Displays NSSA external link states.
Router#**show ip ospf database summary**	Displays a summary of the OSPF database.
Router#**show ip ospf interface**	Displays OSPF info as it relates to all interfaces.
Router#**show ip ospf interface fastethernet 0/0**	Displays OSPF information for interface fastethernet 0/0.
Router#**show ip ospf neighbor**	Lists all OSPF neighbors and their states.
Router#**show ip ospf neighbor detail**	Displays a detailed list of neighbors.
Router#**show ip ospf virtual-links**	Displays information about virtual links.

Troubleshooting OSPF

Router#**clear ip route ***	Clears the entire routing table, forcing it to rebuild.
Router#**clear ip route a.b.c.d**	Clears a specific route to network a.b.c.d.
Router#**clear ip ospf counters**	Resets OSPF counters.
Router#**clear ip ospf process**	Resets the *entire* OSPF process, forcing OSPF to re-create neighbors, database, and routing table.

`Router#debug ip ospf events`	Displays *all* OSPF events.
`Router#debug ip ospf adjacency`	Displays various OSPF states and DR/BDR election between adjacent routers.
`Router#debug ip ospf packets`	Displays OSPF packets.

Configuration Example: Single-Area OSPF

Figure 3-2 shows the network topology for the configuration that follows, which demonstrates how to configure single-area OSPF using the commands covered in this chapter.

Figure 3-2   Network Topology for Single-Area OSPF Configuration

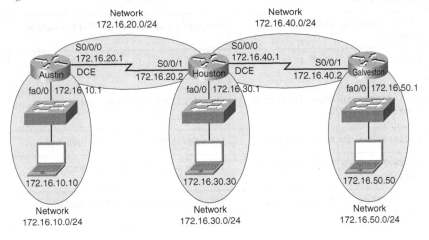

Austin Router

`Router>enable`	Moves to privileged mode.
`Router#configure terminal`	Moves to global configuration mode.
`Router(config)#hostname Austin`	Sets the hostname.
`Austin(config)#interface fastethernet 0/0`	Moves to interface configuration mode.
`Austin(config-if)#ip address 172.16.10.1 255.255.255.0`	Assigns an IP address and netmask.

`Austin(config-if)#no shutdown`	Enables the interface.
`Austin(config-if)#interface serial 0/0/0`	Moves to interface configuration mode.
`Austin(config-if)#ip address 172.16.20.1 255.255.255.252`	Assigns an IP address and netmask.
`Austin(config-if)#clock rate 56000`	Sets a clock rate on this interface. A DCE cable must be plugged in to this side.
`Austin(config-if)#no shutdown`	Enables the interface.
`Austin(config-if)#exit`	Returns to global configuration mode.
`Austin(config)#router ospf 1`	Starts OSPF process 1.
`Austin(config-router)#network 172.16.10.0 0.0.0.255 area 0`	Read this line to say, "Any interface with an address of 172.16.10.x is to be put into area 0."
`Austin(config-router)#network 172.16.20.0 0.0.0.255 area 0`	Read this line to say, "Any interface with an address of 172.16.20.x is to be put into area 0.
`Austin(config-router)#<ctrl> z`	Returns to privileged mode.
`Austin#copy running-config startup-config`	Saves the configuration to NVRAM.

Houston Router

`Router>enable`	Moves to privileged mode.
`Router#configure terminal`	Moves to global configuration mode.
`Router(config)#hostname Houston`	Sets the hostname.
`Houston(config)#interface fastethernet 0/0`	Moves to interface configuration mode.
`Houston(config-if)#ip address 172.16.30.1 255.255.255.0`	Assigns an IP address and netmask.
`Houston(config-if)#no shutdown`	Enables the interface.

Houston(config-if)#interface serial 0/0/0	Moves to interface configuration mode.
Houston(config-if)#ip address 172.16.40.1 255.255.255.252	Assigns an IP address and netmask.
Houston(config-if)#clock rate 56000	Sets a clock rate on this interface. A DCE cable must be plugged in to this side.
Houston(config-if)#no shutdown	Enables the interface.
Houston(config)#interface serial 0/0/1	Moves to interface configuration mode.
Houston(config-if)#ip address 172.16.20.2 255.255.255.252	Assigns an IP address and netmask.
Houston(config-if)#no shutdown	Enables the interface.
Houston(config-if)#exit	Returns to global configuration mode.
Houston(config)#router ospf 1	Starts OSPF process 1.
Houston(config-router)#network 172.16.0.0 0.0.255.255 area 0	Read this line to say, "Any interface with an address of 172.16.x.x is to be put into area 0." One statement will now advertise all three interfaces.
Houston(config-router)#<ctrl> z	Returns to privileged mode.
Houston#copy running-config startup-config	Saves the configuration to NVRAM.

Galveston Router

Router>enable	Moves to privileged mode.
Router#configure terminal	Moves to global configuration mode.
Router(config)#hostname Galveston	Sets the hostname.
Galveston(config)#interface fastethernet 0/0	Moves to interface configuration mode.
Galveston(config-if)#ip address 172.16.50.1 255.255.255.0	Assigns an IP address and netmask.

Galveston(config-if)#**no shutdown**	Enables the interface.
Galveston(config-if)#**interface serial 0/0/1**	Moves to interface configuration mode.
Galveston(config-if)#**ip address 172.16.40.2 255.255.255.252**	Assigns an IP address and netmask.
Galveston(config-if)#**no shutdown**	Enables the interface.
Galveston(config-if)#**exit**	Returns to global configuration mode.
Galveston(config)#**router ospf 1**	Starts OSPF process 1.
Galveston(config-router)#**network 172.16.40.2 0.0.0.0 area 0**	Any interface with an exact address of 172.16.40.2 is to be put into area 0. This is the most precise way to place an exact address into the OSPF routing process.
Galveston(config-router)#**network 172.16.50.1 0.0.0.0 area 0**	Read this line to say, "Any interface with an exact address of 172.16.50.1 is to be put into area 0."
Galveston(config-router)#**<ctrl> z**	Returns to privileged mode.
Galveston#**copy running-config startup-config**	Saves the configuration to NVRAM.

Configuration Example: Multiarea OSPF

Figure 3-3 shows the network topology for the configuration that follows, which demonstrates how to configure multiarea OSPF using the commands covered in this chapter.

Figure 3-3   *Network Topology for Multiarea OSPF Configuration*

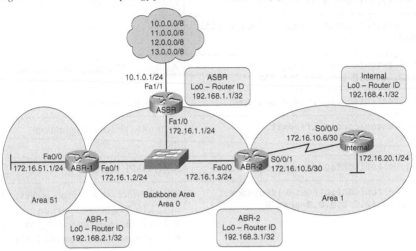

ASBR Router

Router>`enable`	Moves to privileged mode.
Router#`configure terminal`	Moves to global configuration mode.
Router(config)#`hostname ASBR`	Sets the router hostname.
ASBR(config)#`interface loopback 0`	Enters loopback interface mode.
ASBR(config-if)#`ip address 192.168.1.1 255.255.255.255`	Assigns an IP address and netmask.
ASBR(config-if)#`description Router ID`	Sets a locally significant description.
ASBR(config-if)#`exit`	Returns to global configuration mode.
ASBR(config)#`interface fastethernet 0/0`	Enters interface configuration mode.
ASBR(config-if)#`ip address 172.16.1.1 255.255.255.0`	Assigns an IP address and netmask.
ASBR(config-if)#`no shutdown`	Enables the interface.
ASBR(config-if)#`exit`	Returns to global configuration mode.
ASBR(config)#`ip route 0.0.0.0 0.0.0.0 10.1.0.2 fastethernet 0/1`	Creates default route. Using both an exit interface and next-hop address on a Fast Ethernet interface prevents recursive lookups in the routing table.

ASBR(config)#ip route 11.0.0.0 0.0.0.0 null0	Creates a static route to a null interface. In this example, these routes represent a simulated remote destination.
ASBR(config)#ip route 12.0.0.0 0.0.0.0 null0	Creates a static route to a null interface. In this example, these routes represent a simulated remote destination.
ASBR(config)#ip route 13.0.0.0 0.0.0.0 null0	Creates a static route to a null interface. In this example, these routes represent a simulated remote destination.
ASBR(config)#**router ospf 1**	Starts OSPF process 1.
ASBR(config-router)#**network 172.16.1.0 0.0.0.255 area 0**	Read this line to say, "Any interface with an address of 172.16.1.x is to be put into area 0."
ASBR(config-router)#**default-information originate**	Sets the default route to be propagated to all OSPF routers.
ASBR(config-router)#**redistribute static**	Redistributes static routes into the OSPF process. This turns the router into an ASBR because static routes are not part of OSPF, and the definition of an ASBR is a router that sits between OSPF and another routing process—in this case, static routing.
ASBR(config-router)#**exit**	Returns to global configuration mode.
ASBR(config)#**exit**	Returns to privileged mode.
ASBR#**copy running-config startup-config**	Saves the configuration to NVRAM.

ABR-1 Router

Router>**enable**	Moves to privileged mode.
Router#**configure terminal**	Moves to global configuration mode.
Router(config)#**hostname ABR-1**	Sets the router hostname.
ABR-1(config)#**interface loopback 0**	Enters loopback interface mode.
ABR-1(config-if)#**ip address 192.168.2.1 255.255.255.255**	Assigns an IP address and netmask.

ABR-1(config-if)#**description Router ID**	Sets a locally significant description.
ABR-1(config-if)#**exit**	Returns to global configuration mode.
ABR-1(config)#**interface fastethernet 0/1**	Enters interface configuration mode.
ABR-1(config-if)#**ip address 172.16.1.2 255.255.255.0**	Assigns an IP address and netmask.
ABR-1(config-if)#**ip ospf priority 200**	Sets the priority for the DR/BDR election process. This router will win and become the DR.
ABR-1(config-if)#**no shutdown**	Enables the interface.
ABR-1(config-if)#**exit**	Returns to global configuration mode.
ABR-1(config)#**interface fastethernet 0/0**	Enters interface configuration mode.
ABR-1(config-if)#**ip address 172.16.51.1 255.255.255.0**	Assigns an IP address and netmask.
ABR-1(config-if)#**no shutdown**	Enables the interface.
ABR-1(config-if)#**exit**	Returns to global configuration mode.
ABR-1(config)#**router ospf 1**	Starts OSPF process 1.
ABR-1(config-router)#**network 172.16.1.0 0.0.0.255 area 0**	Read this line to say, "Any interface with an address of 172.16.1.x is to be put into area 0."
ABR-1(config-router)#**network 172.16.51.1 0.0.0.0 area 51**	Read this line to say, "Any interface with an exact address of 172.16.51.1 is to be put into area 51."
ABR-1(config-router)#**exit**	Returns to global configuration mode.
ABR-1(config)#**exit**	Returns to privileged mode.
ABR-1(config)#**copy running-config startup-config**	Saves the configuration to NVRAM.

ABR-2 Router

Router>`enable`	Moves to privileged mode.
Router#`configure terminal`	Moves to global configuration mode.
Router(config)#`hostname ABR-2`	Sets the router hostname.
ABR-2(config)#`interface loopback 0`	Enters loopback interface mode.
ABR-2(config-if)#`ip address` `192.168.3.1 255.255.255.255`	Assigns an IP address and netmask.
ABR-2(config-if)#`description Router ID`	Sets a locally significant description.
ABR-2(config-if)#`exit`	Returns to global configuration mode.
ABR-2(config)#`interface fastethernet 0/0`	Enters interface configuration mode.
ABR-2(config-if)#`ip address` `172.16.1.3 255.255.255.0`	Assigns an IP address and netmask.
ABR-2(config-if)#`ip ospf priority 100`	Sets the priority for the DR/BDR election process. This router will become the BDR to ABR-1's DR.
ABR-2(config-if)#`no shutdown`	Enables the interface.
ABR-2(config-if)#`exit`	Returns to global configuration mode.
ABR-2(config)#`interface serial 0/0/1`	Enters interface configuration mode.
ABR-2(config-if)#`ip address` `172.16.10.5 255.255.255.252`	Assigns an IP address and netmask.
ABR-2(config-if)#`clock rate 56000`	Assigns a clock rate to the interface.
ABR-2(config-if)#`no shutdown`	Enables the interface.
ABR-2(config-if)#`exit`	Returns to global configuration mode.
ABR-2(config)#`router ospf 1`	Starts OSPF process 1.
ABR-2(config-router)#`network` `172.16.1.0 0.0.0.255 area 0`	Read this line to say, "Any interface with an address of 172.16.1.x is to be put into area 0."

ABR-2(config-router)#**network 172.16.10.4 0.0.0.3 area 1**	Read this line to say, "Any interface with an address of 172.16.10.4–7 is to be put into area 1."
ABR-2(config-router)#**area 1 stub**	Makes area 1 a stub area. LSA type 4 and type 5s are blocked and not sent into area 1. A default route is injected into the stub area, pointing to the ABR.
ABR-2(config-router)#**exit**	Returns to global configuration mode.
ABR-2(config)#**exit**	Returns to privileged mode.
ABR-2(config)#**copy running-config startup-config**	Saves the configuration to NVRAM.

Internal Router

Router>**enable**	Moves to privileged mode.
Router#**configure terminal**	Moves to global configuration mode.
Router(config)#**hostname Internal**	Sets the router hostname.
Internal(config)#**interface loopback 0**	Enters loopback interface mode.
Internal(config-if)#**ip address 192.168.4.1 255.255.255.255**	Assigns an IP address and netmask.
Internal(config-if)#**description Router ID**	Sets a locally significant description.
Internal(config-if)#**exit**	Returns to global configuration mode.
Internal(config)#**interface fastethernet 0/0**	Enters interface configuration mode.
Internal(config-if)#**ip address 172.16.20.1 255.255.255.0**	Assigns an IP address and netmask.
Internal(config-if)#**no shutdown**	Enables the interface.
Internal(config-if)#**exit**	Returns to global configuration mode.
Internal(config)#**interface serial 0/0/0**	Enters interface configuration mode.
Internal(config-if)#**ip address 172.16.10.6 255.255.255.252**	Assigns an IP address and netmask.
Internal(config-if)#**no shutdown**	Enables the interface.
Internal(config-if)#**exit**	Returns to global configuration mode.

`Internal(config)#router ospf 1`	Starts OSPF process 1.
`Internal(config-router)#network 172.16.0.0 0.0.255.255 area 0`	Read this line to say, "Any interface with an address of 172.16.*x.x* is to be put into area 0."
`Internal(config-router)#area 1 stub`	Makes area 1 a stub area.
`Internal(config-router)#exit`	Returns to global configuration mode.
`Internal(config)#exit`	Returns to privileged mode.
`Internal(config)#copy running-config startup-config`	Saves the configuration to NVRAM.

Configuration Example: OSPF and NBMA Networks

Figure 3-4 shows the network topology for the configuration that follows, which demonstrates how to configure OSPF on an NBMA network using the commands covered in this chapter.

Figure 3-4   Network Topology for OSPF Configuration on an NBMA Network

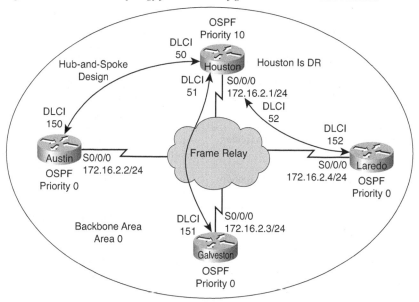

Houston Router

Router>`enable`	Moves to privileged mode.
Router#`configure terminal`	Moves to global configuration mode.
Router(config)#`hostname Houston`	Sets the router hostname.
Houston(config)#`interface serial 0/0/0`	Enters interface configuration mode.
Houston(config-if)#`encapsulation frame-relay`	Enables Frame Relay encapsulation.
Houston(config-if)#`ip address 172.16.2.1 255.255.255.0`	Assigns an IP address and netmask.
Houston(config-if)#`frame-relay map ip 172.16.2.2 50`	Maps the remote IP address to local DLCI 50.
Houston(config-if)#`frame-relay map ip 172.16.2.3 51`	Maps the remote IP address to local DLCI 51.
Houston(config-if)#`frame-relay map ip 172.16.2.4 52`	Maps the remote IP address to local DLCI 52.
Houston(config-if)#`no shutdown`	Enables the interface.
Houston(config-if)#`exit`	Returns to global configuration mode.
Houston(config)#`router ospf 1`	Starts OSPF process 1.
Houston(config-router)#`network 172.16.0.0 0.0.255.255 area 0`	Read this line to say, "Any interface with an IP address of 172.16.x.x will be placed into area 0."
Houston(config-router)#`neighbor 172.16.2.2`	Identifies neighbor (Austin) to Houston.
Houston(config-router)#`neighbor 172.16.2.3`	Identifies neighbor (Galveston) to Houston.
Houston(config-router)#`neighbor 172.16.2.4`	Identifies neighbor (Laredo) to Houston.
Houston(config-router)#`exit`	Returns to global configuration mode
Houston(config)#`exit`	Returns to privileged mode.
Houston#`copy running-config startup-config`	Saves the configuration to NVRAM.

Austin Router

`Router>`**`enable`**	Moves to privileged mode.
`Router#`**`configure terminal`**	Moves to global configuration mode.
`Router(config)#`**`hostname Austin`**	Sets the router hostname.
`Austin(config)#`**`interface serial 0/0/0`**	Enters interface configuration mode.
`Austin(config-if)#`**`encapsulation frame-relay`**	Enables Frame Relay encapsulation.
`Austin(config-if)#`**`ip address 172.16.2.2 255.255.255.0`**	Assigns an IP address and netmask.
`Austin(config-if)#`**`frame-relay map ip 172.16.2.1 150`**	Maps the remote IP address to local DLCI 150.
`Austin(config-if)#`**`frame-relay map ip 172.16.2.3 150`**	Maps the remote IP address to local DLCI 150.
`Austin(config-if)#`**`frame-relay map ip 172.16.2.4 150`**	Maps the remote IP address to local DLCI 150.
`Austin(config-if)#`**`no shutdown`**	Enables the interface.
`Austin(config-if)#`**`exit`**	Returns to global configuration mode.
`Austin(config)#`**`router ospf 1`**	Starts OSPF process 1.
`Austin(config-router)#`**`network 172.16.0.0 0.0.255.255 area 0`**	Read this line to say, "Any interface with an IP address of 172.16.*x*.*x* will be placed into area 0."
`Austin(config-router)#`**`neighbor 172.16.2.1 priority 10`**	Identifies neighbor (Houston) to Austin and assigns a priority of 10 to Houston for DR/BDR election.
`Austin(config-router)#`**`exit`**	Returns to global configuration mode.
`Austin(config)#`**`exit`**	Returns to privileged mode.
`Austin#`**`copy running-config startup-config`**	Saves the configuration to NVRAM.

Galveston Router

Router>`enable`	Moves to privileged mode.
Router#`configure terminal`	Moves to global configuration mode.
Router(config)#`hostname Galveston`	Sets the router hostname.
Galveston(config)#`interface serial 0/0/0`	Enters interface configuration mode.
Galveston(config-if)#`encapsulation frame-relay`	Enables Frame Relay encapsulation.
Galveston(config-if)#`ip address 172.16.2.3 255.255.255.0`	Assigns an IP address and netmask.
Galveston(config-if)#`frame-relay map ip 172.16.2.1 151`	Maps the remote IP address to local DLCI 151.
Galveston(config-if)#`frame-relay map ip 172.16.2.2 151`	Maps the remote IP address to local DLCI 151.
Galveston(config-if)#`frame-relay map ip 172.16.2.4 151`	Maps the remote IP address to local DLCI 151.
Galveston(config-if)#`no shutdown`	Enables the interface.
Galveston(config-if)#`exit`	Returns to global configuration mode.
Galveston(config)#`router ospf 1`	Starts OSPF process 1.
Galveston(config-router)#`network 172.16.0.0 0.0.255.255 area 0`	Read this line to say, "Any interface with an IP address of 172.16.x.x will be placed into area 0."
Galveston(config-router)#`neighbor 172.16.2.1 priority 10`	Identifies neighbor (Houston) to Galveston and assigns a priority of 10 to Houston for DR/BDR election.
Galveston(config-router)#`exit`	Returns to global configuration mode.
Galveston(config)#`exit`	Returns to privileged mode.
Galveston#`copy running-config startup-config`	Saves the configuration to NVRAM.

Laredo Router

`Router>`**`enable`**	Moves to privileged mode.
`Router#`**`configure terminal`**	Moves to global configuration mode.
`Router(config)#`**`hostname Laredo`**	Sets the router hostname.
`Laredo(config)#`**`interface serial 0/0/0`**	Enters interface configuration mode.
`Laredo(config-if)#`**`encapsulation frame-relay`**	Enables Frame Relay encapsulation.
`Laredo(config-if)#`**`ip address 172.16.2.4 255.255.255.0`**	Assigns an IP address and netmask.
`Laredo(config-if)#`**`frame-relay map ip 172.16.2.1 152`**	Maps the remote IP address to local DLCI 152.
`Laredo(config-if)#`**`frame-relay map ip 172.16.2.2 152`**	Maps the remote IP address to local DLCI 152.
`Laredo(config-if)#`**`frame-relay map ip 172.16.2.3 152`**	Maps the remote IP address to local DLCI 152.
`Laredo(config-if)#`**`no shutdown`**	Enables the interface.
`Laredo(config-if)#`**`exit`**	Returns to global configuration mode.
`Laredo(config)#`**`router ospf 1`**	Starts OSPF process 1.
`Laredo(config-router)#`**`network 172.16.0.0 0.0.255.255 area 0`**	Read this line to say, "Any interface with an IP address of 172.16.*x.x* will be placed into area 0."
`Laredo(config-router)#`**`neighbor 172.16.2.1 priority 10`**	Identifies neighbor (Houston) to Laredo and assigns a priority of 10 to Houston for DR/BDR election.
`Laredo(config-router)#`**`exit`**	Returns to global configuration mode.
`Laredo(config)#`**`exit`**	Returns to privileged mode.
`Laredo#`**`copy running-config startup-config`**	Saves the configuration to NVRAM.

Configuration Example: OSPF and Broadcast Networks

Figure 3-5 shows the network topology for the configuration that follows, which demonstrates how to configure OSPF on a broadcast network using the commands covered in this chapter.

Figure 3-5   Network Topology for OSPF Configuration on a Broadcast Network

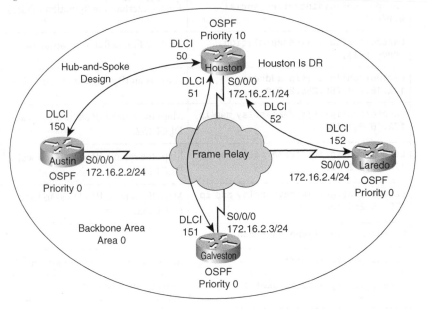

Houston Router

`Router>`**`enable`**	Moves to privileged mode.
`Router#`**`configure terminal`**	Moves to global configuration mode.
`Router(config)#`**`hostname Houston`**	Sets the router hostname.
`Houston(config)#`**`interface serial 0/0/0`**	Enters interface configuration mode.
`Houston(config-if)#`**`encapsulation frame-relay`**	Enables Frame Relay encapsulation.
`Houston(config-if)#`**`ip address 172.16.2.1 255.255.255.0`**	Assigns an IP address and netmask.
`Houston(config-if)#`**`ip ospf network broadcast`**	Changes the network type from the default NBMA to broadcast.

Houston(config-if)#**ip ospf priority 10**	Sets the priority to 10 for the DR/BDR election process.
Houston(config-if)#**frame-relay map ip 172.16.2.2 50 broadcast**	Maps the remote IP address to local DLCI 50. Broadcast and multicasts will now be forwarded.
Houston(config-if)#**frame-relay map ip 172.16.2.3 51 broadcast**	Maps the remote IP address to local DLCI 51. Broadcast and multicasts will now be forwarded.
Houston(config-if)#**frame-relay map ip 172.16.2.4 52 broadcast**	Maps the remote IP address to local DLCI 52. Broadcast and multicasts will now be forwarded.
Houston(config-if)#**no shut**	Enables the interface.
Houston(config-if)#**exit**	Returns to global configuration mode.
Houston(config)#**router ospf 1**	Starts OSPF process 1.
Houston(config-router)#**network 172.16.0.0 0.0.255.255 area 0**	Read this line to say, "Any interface with an IP address of 172.16.*x.x* will be placed into area 0."
Houston(config-router)#**exit**	Returns to global configuration mode.
Houston(config)#**exit**	Returns to privileged mode.
Houston#**copy running-config startup-config**	Saves the configuration to NVRAM.

Austin Router

Router>**enable**	Moves to privileged mode.
Router#**configure terminal**	Moves to global configuration mode.
Router(config)#**hostname Austin**	Sets the router hostname.
Austin(config)#**interface serial 0/0/0**	Enters interface configuration mode.
Austin(config-if)#**encapsulation frame-relay**	Enables Frame Relay encapsulation.
Austin(config-if)#**ip address 172.16.2.2 255.255.255.0**	Assigns an IP address and netmask.

`Austin(config-if)#ip ospf network broadcast`	Changes the network type from the default NBMA to broadcast.
`Austin(config-if)#ip ospf priority 0`	Sets the priority to 0 for the DR/BDR election process. Austin will not participate in the election process.
`Austin(config-if)#frame-relay map ip 172.16.2.1 150 broadcast`	Maps the remote IP address to local DLCI 150. Broadcast and multicasts will now be forwarded.
`Austin(config-if)#frame-relay map ip 172.16.2.3 150 broadcast`	Maps the remote IP address to local DLCI 150. Broadcast and multicasts will now be forwarded.
`Austin(config-if)#frame-relay map ip 172.16.2.4 150 broadcast`	Maps the remote IP address to local DLCI 150. Broadcast and multicasts will now be forwarded.
`Austin(config-if)#no shutdown`	Enables the interface.
`Austin(config-if)#exit`	Returns to global configuration mode.
`Austin(config)#router ospf 1`	Starts OSPF process 1.
`Austin(config-router)#network 172.16.0.0 0.0.255.255 area 0`	Read this line to say, "Any interface with an IP address of 172.16.*x*.*x* will be placed into area 0."
`Austin(config-router)#exit`	Returns to global configuration mode.
`Austin(config)#exit`	Returns to privileged mode.
`Austin#copy running-config startup-config`	Saves the configuration to NVRAM.

Galveston Router

`Router>enable`	Moves to privileged mode.
`Router#configure terminal`	Moves to global configuration mode.
`Router(config)#hostname Galveston`	Sets the router hostname.
`Galveston(config)#interface serial 0/0/0`	Enters interface configuration mode.
`Galveston(config-if)#encapsulation frame-relay`	Enables Frame Relay encapsulation.

Galveston(config-if)#**ip address 172.16.2.3 255.255.255.0**	Assigns an IP address and netmask.
Galveston(config-if)#**ip ospf network broadcast**	Changes the network type from the default NBMA to broadcast.
Galveston(config-if)#**ip ospf priority 0**	Sets the priority to 0 for the DR/BDR election process. Galveston will not participate in the election process.
Galveston(config-if)#**frame-relay map ip 172.16.2.1 151 broadcast**	Maps the remote IP address to local DLCI 151. Broadcast and multicasts will now be forwarded.
Galveston(config-if)#**frame-relay map ip 172.16.2.2 151 broadcast**	Maps the remote IP address to local DLCI 151. Broadcast and multicasts will now be forwarded.
Galveston(config-if)#**frame-relay map ip 172.16.2.4 151 broadcast**	Maps the remote IP address to local DLCI 151. Broadcast and multicasts will now be forwarded.
Galveston(config-if)#**no shutdown**	Enables the interface.
Galveston(config-if)#**exit**	Returns to global configuration mode.
Galveston(config)#**router ospf 1**	Starts OSPF process 1.
Galveston(config-router)#**network 172.16.0.0 0.0.255.255 area 0**	Read this line to say, "Any interface with an IP address of 172.16.*x.x* will be placed into area 0."
Galveston(config-router)#**exit**	Returns to global configuration mode.
Galveston(config)#**exit**	Returns to privileged mode.
Galveston#**copy running-config startup-config**	Saves the configuration to NVRAM.

Laredo Router

Router>**enable**	Moves to privileged mode.
Router#**configure terminal**	Moves to global configuration mode.
Router(config)#**hostname Laredo**	Sets the router hostname.
Laredo(config)#**interface serial 0/0/0**	Enters interface configuration mode.

`Laredo(config-if)#encapsulation frame-relay`	Enables Frame Relay encapsulation.
`Laredo(config-if)#ip address 172.16.2.4 255.255.255.0`	Assigns an IP address and netmask.
`Laredo(config-if)#ip ospf network broadcast`	Changes the network type from the default NBMA to broadcast.
`Laredo(config-if)#ip ospf priority 0`	Sets the priority to 0 for the DR/BDR election process. Laredo will not participate in the election process.
`Laredo(config-if)#frame-relay map ip 172.16.2.1 152 broadcast`	Maps the remote IP address to local DLCI 152. Broadcast and multicasts will now be forwarded.
`Laredo(config-if)#frame-relay map ip 172.16.2.2 152 broadcast`	Maps the remote IP address to local DLCI 152. Broadcast and multicasts will now be forwarded.
`Laredo(config-if)#frame-relay map ip 172.16.2.3 152 broadcast`	Maps the remote IP address to local DLCI 152. Broadcast and multicasts will now be forwarded.
`Laredo(config-if)#no shutdown`	Enables the interface.
`Laredo(config-if)#exit`	Returns to global configuration mode.
`Laredo(config)#router ospf 1`	Starts OSPF process 1.
`Laredo(config-router)#network 172.16.0.0 0.0.255.255 area 0`	Read this line to say, "Any interface with an IP address of 172.16.$x.x$ will be placed into area 0."
`Laredo(config-router)#exit`	Returns to global configuration mode.
`Laredo(config)#exit`	Returns to privileged mode.
`Laredo#copy running-config startup-config`	Saves the configuration to NVRAM.

Configuration Example: OSPF and Point-to-Multipoint Networks

Figure 3-6 shows the network topology for the configuration that follows, which demonstrates how to configure OSPF on a point-to-multipoint network using the commands covered in this chapter.

Figure 3-6   *Network Topology for OSPF Configuration on a Point-to-Multipoint Network*

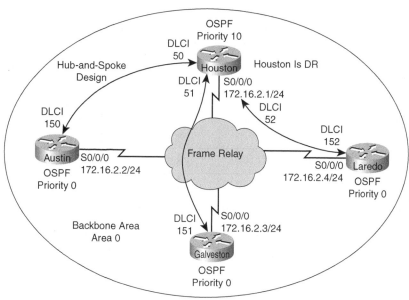

Houston Router

Router>`enable`	Moves to privileged mode.
Router#`configure terminal`	Moves to privileged mode.
Router(config)#`hostname Houston`	Sets the router hostname.
Houston(config)#`interface serial 0/0/0`	Enters interface configuration mode.
Houston(config-if)#`encapsulation frame-relay`	Enables Frame Relay encapsulation.
Houston(config-if)#`ip address 172.16.2.1 255.255.255.0`	Assigns an IP address and netmask.
Houston(config-if)#`ip ospf network point-to-multipoint`	Changes the network type from the default NBMA to point-to-multipoint.
Houston(config-if)#`frame-relay map ip 172.16.2.2 50`	Maps the remote IP address to local DLCI 50.
Houston(config-if)#`frame-relay map ip 172.16.2.3 51`	Maps the remote IP address to local DLCI 51.

`Houston(config-if)#frame-relay map ip 172.16.2.4 52`	Maps the remote IP address to local DLCI 52.
`Houston(config-if)#no shutdown`	Enables the interface.
`Houston(config-if)#exit`	Returns to global configuration mode.
`Houston(config)#router ospf 1`	Enables OSPF process 1.
`Houston(config-router)#network 172.16.0.0 0.0.255.255 area 0`	Read this line to say, "Any interface with an IP address of 172.16.$x.x$ will be placed into area 0."
`Houston(config-router)#exit`	Returns to global configuration mode.
`Houston(config)#exit`	Returns to privileged mode.
`Houston#copy running-config startup-config`	Saves the configuration to NVRAM.

Austin Router

`Router>enable`	Moves to privileged mode.
`Router#configure terminal`	Moves to global configuration mode.
`Router(config)#hostname Austin`	Sets the router hostname.
`Austin(config)#interface serial 0/0/0`	Enters serial interface mode.
`Austin(config-if)#encapsulation frame-relay`	Enables Frame Relay encapsulation.
`Austin(config-if)#ip address 172.16.2.2 255.255.255.0`	Assigns an IP address and netmask.
`Austin(config-if)#ip ospf network point-to-multipoint`	Changes the network type from the default NBMA to point-to-multipoint.
`Austin(config-if)#frame-relay map ip 172.16.2.1 150`	Maps the remote IP address to local DLCI 150.
`Austin(config-if)#frame-relay map ip 172.16.2.3 150`	Maps the remote IP address to local DLCI 150.
`Austin(config-if)#frame-relay map ip 172.16.2.4 150`	Maps the remote IP address to local DLCI 150.

`Austin(config-if)#no shutdown`	Enables the interface.
`Austin(config-if)#exit`	Returns to global configuration mode.
`Austin(config)#router ospf 1`	Starts OSPF process 1.
`Austin(config-router)#network 172.16.0.0 0.0.255.255 area 0`	Read this line to say, "Any interface with an IP address of 172.16.$x.x$ will be placed into area 0."
`Austin(config-router)#exit`	Returns to global configuration mode.
`Austin(config)#exit`	Returns to privileged mode.
`Austin#copy running-config startup-config`	Saves the configuration to NVRAM.

Galveston Router

`Router>enable`	Moves to privileged mode.
`Router#configure terminal`	Moves to global configuration mode.
`Router(config)#hostname Galveston`	Sets the router hostname.
`Galveston(config)#interface serial 0/0/0`	Enters interface configuration mode.
`Galveston(config-if)#encapsulation frame-relay`	Enables Frame Relay encapsulation.
`Galveston(config-if)#ip address 172.16.2.3 255.255.255.0`	Assigns an IP address and netmask.
`Galveston(config-if)#ip ospf network point-to-multipoint`	Changes the network type from the default NBMA to point-to-multipoint.
`Galveston(config-if)#frame-relay map ip 172.16.2.1 151`	Maps the remote IP address to local DLCI 151.
`Galveston(config-if)#frame-relay map ip 172.16.2.2 151`	Maps the remote IP address to local DLCI 151.
`Galveston(config-if)#frame-relay map ip 172.16.2.4 151`	Maps the remote IP address to local DLCI 151.
`Galveston(config-if)#no shutdown`	Enables the interface.

`Galveston(config-if)#exit`	Returns to global configuration mode.
`Galveston(config)#router ospf 1`	Starts OSPF process 1.
`Galveston(config-router)#network 172.16.0.0 0.0.255.255 area 0`	Read this line to say, "Any interface with an IP address of 172.16.x.x will be placed into area 0."
`Galveston(config-router)#exit`	Returns to global configuration mode.
`Galveston(config)#exit`	Returns to privileged mode.
`Galveston#copy running-config startup-config`	Saves the configuration to NVRAM.

Laredo Router

`Router>enable`	Moves to privileged mode.
`Router#configure terminal`	Moves to global configuration mode.
`Router(config)#hostname Laredo`	Sets the router hostname.
`Laredo(config)#interface serial 0/0/0`	Enters interface configuration mode.
`Laredo(config-if)#encapsulation frame-relay`	Enables Frame Relay encapsulation.
`Laredo(config-if)#ip address 172.16.2.4 255.255.255.0`	Assigns an IP address and netmask.
`Laredo(config-if)#ip ospf network point-to-multipoint`	Changes the network type from the default NBMA to point-to-multipoint.
`Laredo(config-if)#frame-relay map ip 172.16.2.1 152`	Maps the remote IP address to local DLCI 152.
`Laredo(config-if)#frame-relay map ip 172.16.2.2 152`	Maps the remote IP address to local DLCI 152.
`Laredo(config-if)#frame-relay map ip 172.16.2.3 152`	Maps the remote IP address to local DLCI 152.
`Laredo(config-if)#no shutdown`	Enables the interface.
`Laredo(config-if)#exit`	Returns to global configuration mode.

`Laredo(config)#`**`router ospf 1`**	Starts OSPF process 1.
`Laredo(config-router)#`**`network`** **`172.16.0.0 0.0.255.255 area 0`**	Read this line to say, "Any interface with an IP address of 172.16.*x.x* will be placed into area 0."
`Laredo(config-router)#`**`exit`**	Returns to global configuration mode.
`Laredo(config)#`**`exit`**	Returns to privileged mode.
`Laredo#`**`copy running-config startup-config`**	Saves the configuration to NVRAM.

Configuration Example: OSPF and Point-to-Point Networks Using Subinterfaces

Figure 3-7 shows the network topology for the configuration that follows, which demonstrates how to configure OSPF on a point-to-point network using subinterfaces, using the commands covered in this chapter.

Figure 3-7   *Network Topology for OSPF Configuration on a Point-to-Point Network Using Subinterfaces*

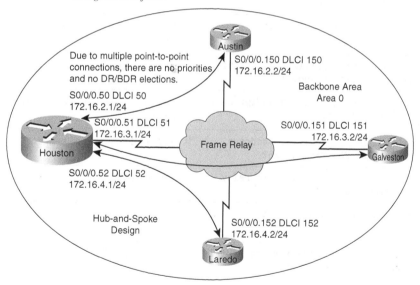

Houston Router

`Router>`**`enable`**	Moves to privileged mode.
`Router#`**`configure terminal`**	Moves to global configuration mode.
`Router(config)#`**`hostname Houston`**	Sets the router hostname.
`Houston(config)#`**`interface serial 0/0/0`**	Enters interface configuration mode.
`Houston(config-if)#`**`encapsulation frame-relay`**	Enables Frame Relay encapsulation.
`Houston(config-if)#`**`no shutdown`**	Enables the interface.
`Houston(config-if)#`**`interface serial 0/0/0.50 point-to-point`**	Creates a subinterface.
`Houston(config-subif)#`**`description Link to Austin`**	Creates a locally significant description of the interface.
`Houston(config-subif)#`**`ip address 172.16.2.1 255.255.255.252`**	Assigns an IP address and netmask.
`Houston(config-subif)#`**`frame-relay interface-dlci 50`**	Assigns a DLCI to the subinterface.
`Houston(config-subif)#`**`exit`**	Returns to interface configuration mode.
`Houston(config-if)#`**`interface serial 0/0/0.51 point-to-point`**	Creates a subinterface.
`Houston(config-subif)#`**`description Link to Galveston`**	Creates a locally significant description of the interface.
`Houston(config-subif)#`**`ip address 172.16.3.1 255.255.255.252`**	Assigns an IP address and netmask.
`Houston(config-subif)#`**`frame-relay interface-dlci 51`**	Assigns a DLCI to the subinterface.
`Houston(config-subif)#`**`exit`**	Returns to interface configuration mode.
`Houston(config-if)#`**`interface serial 0/0/0.52 point-to-point`**	Creates a subinterface.
`Houston(config-subif)#`**`description Link to Laredo`**	Creates a locally significant description of the interface.

Houston(config-subif)#`ip address 172.16.4.1 255.255.255.252`	Assigns an IP address and netmask.
Houston(config-subif)#`frame-relay interface-dlci 52`	Assigns a DLCI to the subinterface.
Houston(config-subif)#`exit`	Returns to interface configuration mode.
Houston(config-if)#`exit`	Returns to global configuration mode.
Houston(config)#`router ospf 1`	Starts OSPF process 1.
Houston(config-router)#`network 172.16.0.0 0.0.255.255 area 0`	Read this line to say, "Any interface with an IP address of 172.16.x.x will be placed into area 0."
Houston(config-router)#`exit`	Returns to global configuration mode.
Houston(config)#`exit`	Returns to privileged mode.
Houston#`copy running-config startup-config`	Saves the configuration to NVRAM.

Austin Router

Router>`enable`	Moves to privileged mode.
Router#`configure terminal`	Moves to global configuration mode.
Router(config)#`hostname Austin`	Sets the router hostname.
Austin(config)#`interface serial 0/0/0`	Enters interface configuration mode.
Austin(config-if)#`encapsulation frame-relay`	Enables Frame Relay encapsulation.
Austin(config-if)#`no shutdown`	Enables the interface.
Austin(config-if)#`interface serial 0/0/0.150 point-to-point`	Creates a subinterface.
Austin(config-subif)#`description Link to Houston`	Creates a locally significant description of the interface.
Austin(config-subif)#`ip address 172.16.2.2 255.255.255.252`	Assigns an IP address and netmask.
Austin(config-subif)#`frame-relay interface-dlci 150`	Assigns a DLCI to the subinterface.

`Austin(config-subif)#exit`	Returns to interface configuration mode.
`Austin(config-if)#exit`	Returns to global configuration mode.
`Austin(config)#router ospf 1`	Starts OSPF process 1.
`Austin(config-router)#network` `172.16.0.0 0.0.255.255 area 0`	Read this line to say, "Any interface with an IP address of 172.16.x.x will be placed into area 0."
`Austin(config-router)#exit`	Returns to global configuration mode.
`Austin(config)#exit`	Returns to privileged mode.
`Austin#copy running-config startup-` `config`	Saves the configuration to NVRAM.

Galveston Router

`Router>enable`	Moves to privileged mode.
`Router#configure terminal`	Moves to global configuration mode.
`Router(config)#hostname Galveston`	Sets the router hostname.
`Galveston(config)#interface serial` `0/0/0`	Enters interface configuration mode.
`Galveston(config-if)#encapsulation` `frame-relay`	Enables Frame Relay encapsulation.
`Galveston(config-if)#no shutdown`	Enables the interface.
`Galveston(config-if)#interface` `serial 0/0/0.151 point-to-point`	Creates a subinterface.
`Galveston(config-subif)#description` `Link to Houston`	Creates a locally significant description of the interface.
`Galveston(config-subif)#ip address` `172.16.3.2 255.255.255.252`	Assigns an IP address and netmask.
`Galveston(config-subif)#frame-relay` `interface-dlci 151`	Assigns a DLCI to the subinterface.
`Galveston(config-subif)#exit`	Returns to interface configuration mode.
`Galveston(config-if)#exit`	Returns to global configuration mode.

Galveston(config)#**router ospf 1**	Starts OSPF process 1.
Galveston(config-router)#**network 172.16.0.0 0.0.255.255 area 0**	Read this line to say, "Any interface with an IP address of 172.16.*x.x* will be placed into area 0."
Galveston(config-router)#**exit**	Returns to global configuration mode.
Galveston(config)#**exit**	Returns to privileged mode.
Galveston#**copy running-config startup-config**	Saves the configuration to NVRAM.

Laredo Router

Router>**enable**	Moves to privileged mode.
Router#**configure terminal**	Moves to global configuration mode.
Router(config)#**hostname Laredo**	Sets the router hostname.
Laredo(config)#**interface serial 0/0/0**	Enters interface configuration mode.
Laredo(config-if)#**encapsulation frame-relay**	Enables Frame Relay encapsulation.
Laredo(config-if)#**no shutdown**	Enables the interface.
Laredo(config-if)#**interface serial 0/0/0.152 point-to-point**	Creates a subinterface.
Laredo(config-subif)#**description Link to Houston**	Creates a locally significant description of the interface.
Laredo(config-subif)#**ip address 172.16.4.2 255.255.255.252**	Assigns an IP address and netmask.
Laredo(config-subif)#**frame-relay interface-dlci 152**	Assigns a DLCI to the subinterface.
Laredo(config-subif)#**exit**	Returns to interface configuration mode.
Laredo(config-if)#**exit**	Returns to global configuration mode.
Laredo(config)#**router ospf 1**	Starts OSPF process 1.

Laredo(config-router)#**network 172.16.0.0 0.0.255.255 area 0**	Read this line to say, "Any interface with an IP address of 172.16.x.x will be placed into area 0."
Laredo(config-router)#**exit**	Returns to global configuration mode.
Laredo(config)#**exit**	Returns to privileged mode.
Laredo#**copy running-config startup-config**	Saves the configuration to NVRAM.

This chapter provides information concerning the following IPv4-based redistribution topics:

- Route filtering using the **distribute-list** command
- Verifying route filters
- Configuration example: outbound route filters
- Configuration example: inbound route filters
- Using a distribute list that references a prefix list
- Using a distribute list that references a route map
- Route filtering using prefix lists
- Policy routing using route maps
- Configuration example: route maps
- Passive interfaces
- Route redistribution
  - Assigning metrics
  - Redistributing subnets
  - Assigning E1 or E2 routes in OSPF
  - Defining seed metrics
  - Redistributing static routes
  - Redistributing OSPF internal and external routes
  - Using route maps with route redistribution and route tags to prevent routing loops
  - Verifying route redistribution
- Administrative distances
- Static routes: **permanent** keyword
- Floating static routes
- Static routes and recursive lookups

Route Filtering Using the distribute-list Command

`Router(config)#router eigrp 10`	Starts the EIGRP routing process for autonomous system 10.
`Router(config-router)#distribute-list 1 in`	Creates an incoming global distribute list that refers to access control list (ACL) 1.
`Router(config-router)#distribute-list 2 out`	Creates an outgoing global distribute list that refers to ACL 2.
`Router(config-router)#distribute-list 3 in fastethernet 0/0`	Creates an incoming distribute list for interface FastEthernet 0/0 and refers to ACL 3.
`Router(config-router)#distribute-list 4 out serial 0/0/0`	Creates an outgoing distribute list for interface serial 0/0/0 and refers to ACL 4.

Verifying Route Filters

`Router#show ip protocols`	Displays the parameters and current state of active routing protocols.

`Routing Protocol is "eigrp 10"`
  `Outgoing update filter list for all interfaces is 2`
    `Serial 0/0/0 filtered by 4`
  `Incoming update filter list for all interfaces is 1`
    `FastEthernet0/0 filtered by 3`	

NOTE: For each interface and routing process, Cisco IOS permits the following:

- One incoming global distribute list
- One outgoing global distribute list
- One incoming interface distribute list
- One outgoing interface distribute list

CAUTION: Route filters have *no* effect on link-state advertisements (LSA) or the link-state database (LSDB)—a basic requirement of link-state routing protocols is that routers in an area must have identical LSDBs.

NOTE: A route filter can influence the routing table of the router on which the filter is configured but has no effect on the route entries of neighboring routers.

NOTE: OSPF routes *cannot* be filtered from entering the OSPF database. The **distribute-list in** command filters routes only from entering the routing table, but it doesn't prevent link-state packets (LSP) from being propagated.

The command **distribute-list out** works only on the routes being redistributed by the Autonomous System Boundary Routers (ASBR) into OSPF. It can be applied to external Type 2 and external Type 1 routes but *not* to intra-area and interarea routes.

Configuration Example: Outbound Route Filters

Figure 4-1 shows the network topology for the configuration that follows, which demonstrates how to configure outbound route filters to control routing updates using the commands covered in this chapter.

Figure 4-1   Network Topology for Outbound Route Filter Configuration

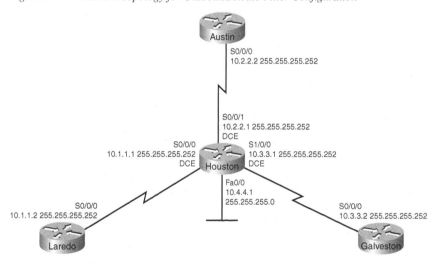

The objective is to prevent subnet 10.1.1.0 from entering Galveston in any EIGRP update from Houston.

Houston Router

| Router>**enable** | Moves to privileged mode. |

`Router#configure terminal`	Moves to global configuration mode.
`Router(config)#hostname Houston`	Assigns a locally significant hostname to the router.
`Houston(config)#interface serial 0/0/0`	Moves to interface configuration mode.
`Houston(config-if)#ip address 10.1.1.1 255.255.255.252`	Configures an IP address and netmask.
`Houston(config-if)#clock rate 56000`	Sets the clock rate for the interface.
`Houston(config-if)#no shutdown`	Enables the interface.
`Houston(config-if)#interface serial 0/0/1`	Moves to interface configuration mode.
`Houston(config-if)#ip address 10.2.2.1 255.255.255.252`	Configures an IP address and netmask.
`Houston(config-if)#no shutdown`	Enables the interface.
`Houston(config-if)#interface serial 1/0/0`	Moves to interface configuration mode.
`Houston(config-if)#ip address 10.3.3.1 255.255.255.252`	Configures an IP address and netmask.
`Houston(config-if)#clock rate 56000`	Sets the clock rate for the interface.
`Houston(config-if)#no shutdown`	Enables the interface.
`Houston(config-if)#interface fastethernet 0/0`	Moves to interface configuration mode.
`Houston(config-if)#ip address 10.4.4.1 255.255.255.0`	Configures an IP address and netmask.
`Houston(config-if)#no shutdown`	Enables the interface.
`Houston(config-if)#exit`	Returns to global configuration mode.
`Houston(config)#router eigrp 10`	Enables the EIGRP routing process for autonomous system 10.
`Houston(config-router)#network 10.0.0.0`	Advertises network 10.0.0.0.

`Houston(config-router)#`**`distribute-list`** **`2 out`**	Creates an outgoing global distribute list that refers to ACL 2.
Or	
`Houston(config-router)#`**`distribute-list`** **`2 out serial 1/0/0`**	Creates an outgoing distribute list for interface serial 1/0/0 that refers to ACL 2.
`Houston(config-router)#`**`exit`**	Returns to global configuration mode.
`Houston(config)#`**`access-list 2 deny`** **`10.1.1.0 0.0.0.255`**	Read this line to say, "All routing updates with an address of 10.1.1.x will be denied and not sent out, based on the parameters of distribute list 2."
`Houston(config)#`**`access-list 2 permit`** **`any`**	Read this line to say, "All routing updates will be permitted to be sent out, based on the parameters of distribute list 2."

If the first **distribute-list** command is used, the EIGRP entry for 10.1.1.0 will not be sent out *any* interface. If the second **distribute-list** command is used, the EIGRP entry for 10.1.1.0 will not be sent out interface serial 1/0/0 but will be sent out other interfaces as per the rules of EIGRP updates.

Configuration Example: Inbound Route Filters

Figure 4-2 shows the network topology for the configuration that follows, which shows how to configure inbound route filters to control routing updates using the commands covered in this chapter.

Figure 4-2   Network Topology for Inbound Route Filter Configuration

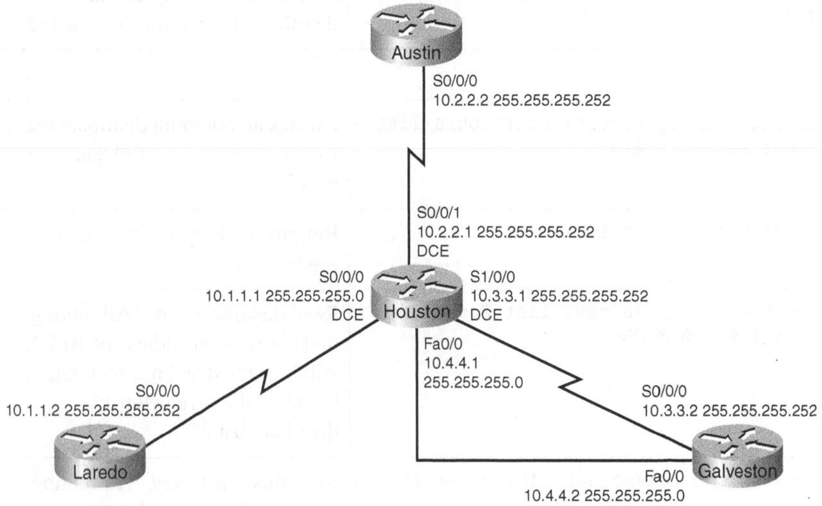

The objective is to prevent subnet 10.1.1.0 from entering Galveston in any EIGRP update from Houston.

Galveston Router

`Router>`**`enable`**	Moves to privileged mode.
`Router#`**`configure terminal`**	Moves to global configuration mode.
`Router(config)#`**`hostname Galveston`**	Sets the router hostname.
`Galveston(config)#`**`interface serial 0/0/0`**	Moves to interface configuration mode.
`Galveston(config-if)#`**`ip address 10.3.3.2 255.255.255.252`**	Assigns an IP address and netmask.
`Galveston(config-if)#`**`interface fastethernet 0/0`**	Moves to interface configuration mode.
`Galveston(config-if)#`**`ip address 10.4.4.2 255.255.255.0`**	Assigns an IP address and netmask.
`Galveston(config-if)#`**`exit`**	Returns to global configuration mode.
`Galveston(config-router)#`**`network 10.0.0.0`**	Advertises network 10.0.0.0.
`Galveston(config-router)#`**`distribute-list 1 in`**	Creates an incoming global distribute list that refers to ACL 1.

Or	
Galveston(config-router)#**distribute-list 1 in serial 0/0/0**	Creates an incoming distribute list for interface s0/0/0 and refers to ACL 1.
Galveston(config-router)#**exit**	Returns to global configuration mode.
Galveston(config)#**access-list 1 deny 10.1.1.0 0.0.0.255**	Read this line to say, "All routing updates with an address of 10.1.1.*x* will be denied and not processed based on the parameters of distribute list 1."
Galveston(config)#**access-list 1 permit any**	Read this line to say, "All routing updates will be permitted based on the parameters of distribute list 1."

If the first **distribute-list** command is used, the EIGRP entry for 10.1.1.0 will be filtered out of the routing update from Houston on *all* interfaces. If the second **distribute-list** command is used, the EIGRP entry for 10.1.1.0 will be filtered out from the routing update received on interface serial 0/0/0, but the entry will be allowed through interface fastethernet 0/0.

Using a Distribute List that References a Prefix List

The following commands show using a distribute list that references a prefix list that will deny /30 networks from leaving interface serial 0/0/1.

Router(config)#**router eigrp 1**	Turns on EIGRP with an autonomous system number of 1 and enters router configuration mode.
Router(config-router)#**distribute-list prefix no-slash30 out serial 0/0/1**	Creates a distribute list applied in an outbound direction on interface serial 0/0/1. This distribute list references a prefix list named no-slash30.
Router(config-router)#**exit**	Returns to global configuration mode.

Router(config)#ip prefix-list no-slash30 seq 15 deny 0.0.0.0/0 ge 30 le 30	Creates a prefix list with a sequence number of 15 and named no-slash30. This prefix list denies any network with a netmask that equals 30.
Router(config)#ip prefix-list no-slash30 seq 20 permit 0.0.0.0/0 le 32	Creates a second line—sequence number 20—in the prefix list named no-slash30. This line will permit all other network entries with masks less than or equal to 32—all other networks.

Using a Distribute List that References a Route Map

The following commands show using a distribute list that references a route map that will deny /30 networks from leaving the router. The route map further references a prefix list.

Router(config)#**router eigrp 1**	Turns on EIGRP with an autonomous system number of 1 and enters router configuration mode.
Router(config-router)#**distribute-list route-map filter-slash30 out**	Creates a distribute list applied in an outbound direction on all interfaces. This distribute list references a route map named filter-slash30.
Router(config-router)#**exit**	Returns to global configuration mode.
Router(config)#**route-map filter-slash30 deny 15**	Creates a route map named filter-slash30. This route map will deny traffic based on subsequent criteria. A sequence number of 15 is assigned.
Router(config-route-map)#**match ip address prefix-list slash30**	Specifies the match criteria (the conditions that should be tested); in this case, match addresses filtered using a prefix list named slash30.
Router(config-route-map)#**exit**	Returns to global configuration mode.

Router(config)#**route-map filter-slash30 permit 23**	Creates a second line for the route map named filter-slash30. This route map will permit traffic based on subsequent criteria. A sequence number of 23 is assigned.
Router(config-route-map)#**exit**	Returns to global configuration mode. Because there is no criteria defined in this line, all traffic will be permitted.
Router(config)#**ip prefix-list slash30 seq 5 permit 0.0.0.0/0 ge 30 le 30**	Creates a prefix list with a sequence number of 5 and named slash30. This prefix list filters any network with a netmask that equals 30.
	NOTE: The decision to filter a route or allow the route through is based on the **deny** or **permit** in the **route-map** command, and *not* the deny or permit in an ACL or prefix list.

Route Filtering Using Prefix Lists

The general syntax for configuring a prefix list is as follows:

Router(config)#**ip prefix-list** *list-name* [**seq** *seq-value*] **deny**|**permit** *network*/*len* [**ge** *ge-value*] [**le** *le-value*]

The following table describes the parameters for this command.

Parameter	Description
list-name	The name of the prefix list.
seq	(Optional) Applies a sequence number to the entry being created or deleted.
seq-value	(Optional) Specifies the sequence number.
deny	Denies access to matching conditions.

permit	Permits access for matching conditions.
network/len	(Mandatory) The network number and length (in bits) of the netmask.
ge	(Optional) Applies *ge-value* to the range specified.
ge-value	(Optional) Specifies the lesser value of a range (the "from" portion of the range description).
le	(Optional) Applies *le-value* to the range specified.
le-value	(Optional) Specifies the greater value of a range (the "to" portion of the range description).

TIP: You must define a prefix list before you can apply it as a route filter.

TIP: There is an **implicit deny** statement at the end of each prefix list.

TIP: The range of sequence numbers that can be entered is from 1 to 4,294,967,294. If a sequence number is not entered when configuring this command, a default sequence numbering is applied to the prefix list. The number 5 is applied to the first prefix entry, and subsequent unnumbered entries are incremented by 5.

TIP: A router tests for prefix list matches from the lowest sequence number to the highest.

By numbering your **prefix-list** statements, you can add new entries at any point in the list.

The following examples show how you can use the **prefix-list** command to filter networks from being propagated through BGP.

Router(config)#**ip prefix-list** KA-TET **permit 172.16.0.0/16**	Creates an IP prefix list for BGP route filtering.
Router(config)#**router bgp 100**	Starts the BGP routing process.
Router(config-router)#**neighbor 192.168.1.1 remote-as 200**	Identifies a peer router at 192.168.1.1.

`Router(config-router)#neighbor 192.168.1.1 prefix-list KA-TET out`	Applies the prefix list named KA-TET to updates sent to this peer.
	This configuration restricts the update to the 172.16.0.0/16 summary. The router will not send a subnet route—such as 172.16.0.0/17 or 172.16.20/24—in an update to autonomous system 200.

The following examples show how you can use the **prefix-list** command to filter networks using some of the more commonly used options.

`Router(config)#ip prefix-list ROSE permit 192.0.0.0/8 le 24`	Creates a prefix list that will accept a netmask of up to 24 bits (**le** meaning less than or equal to) in routes with the prefix 192.0.0.0/8. Because no sequence number is identified, the default number of 5 is applied.
`Router(config)#ip prefix-list ROSE deny 192.0.0.0/8 ge 25`	Creates a prefix list that will deny routes with a netmask of 25 bits or greater (**ge** meaning greater than or equal to) in routes with the prefix 192.0.0.0/8. Because no sequence number is identified, the number 10 is applied—an increment of 5 over the previous statement.
	This configuration will permit routes such as 192.2.0.0/16 or 192.2.20.0/24, but will deny a more specific subnet such as 192.168.10.128/25.
`Router(config)#ip prefix-list TOWER permit 10.0.0.0/8 ge 16 le 24`	Creates a prefix list that permits all prefixes in the 10.0.0.0/8 address space that have a netmask of between 16 and 24 bits (greater than or equal to 16 bits, and less than or equal to 24 bits).
`Router(config)#ip prefix-list SHARDIK seq 5 deny 0.0.0.0/0`	Creates a prefix list and assigns a sequence number of 5 to this statement.

`Router(config)#ip prefix-list SHARDIK` `seq 10 permit 172.16.0.0/16`	Creates a prefix list and assigns a sequence number of 10 to this statement.
`Router(config)#ip prefix-list SHARDIK` `seq 15 permit 192.168.0.0/16 le 24`	Creates a prefix list and assigns a sequence number of 15 to this statement.
`Router(config)#no ip prefix-list` `SHARDIK seq 10`	Removes sequence number 10 from the prefix list.

Policy Routing Using Route Maps

`Router(config)#route-map ISP1` `permit 20`	Creates a route map named ISP1. This route map will permit traffic based on subsequent criteria. A sequence number of 20 is assigned.
	NOTE: In route maps, the default action is to permit.
	NOTE: The *sequence-number* indicates what position the route map is to have in a list of route maps configured with the same name. If no sequence number is given, the first condition in the route map is automatically numbered as 10.
`Router(config-route-map)#match ip` `address 1`	Specifies the match criteria (the conditions that should be tested); in this case, match addresses filtered using ACL 1.
`Router(config-route-map)#set` `interface serial 0/0/0`	Specifies the set actions (what action is to be performed if the match criteria is met); in this case, forward packets out interface serial 0/0/0.
`Router(config-route-map)#exit`	Returns to global configuration mode.
`Router(config)#interface` `fastethernet 0/0`	Moves to interface configuration mode.
`Router(config-if)#ip policy route-` `map ISP1`	Applies the route map to the appropriate LAN interface.

Configuration Example: Route Maps

Figure 4-3 shows the network topology for the configuration that follows, which demonstrates how to configure route maps using the commands covered in this chapter.

Figure 4-3   Network Topology for Route Map Configuration

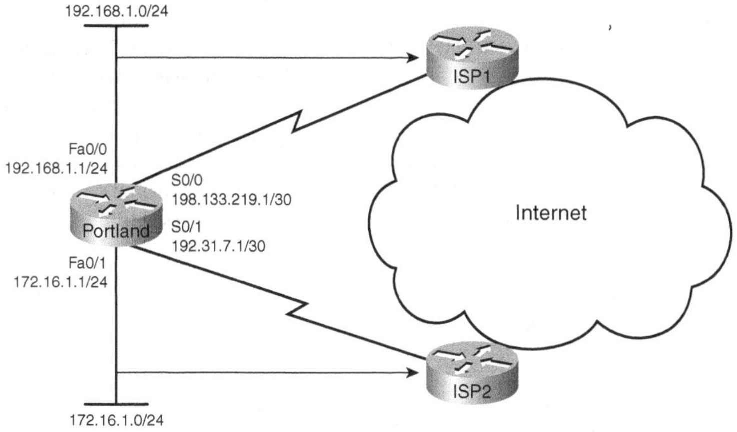

Assume for this example that the policy we want to enforce is this:

- Internet-bound traffic from 192.168.1.0/24 is to be routed to ISP1.
- Internet-bound traffic from 172.16.1.0/24 is to be routed to ISP2.
- All other traffic to be routed normally according to their destination addresses.

Portland Router

Router>`enable`	Moves to privileged mode.
Router#`configure terminal`	Moves to global configuration mode.
Router(config)#`hostname Portland`	Sets the hostname of this router.
Portland(config)#`access-list 1 permit 192.168.1.0 0.0.0.255`	Creates ACL 1, which will filter out addresses for our first route map.
Portland(config)#`access-list 2 permit 172.16.1.0 0.0.0.255`	Creates ACL 2, which will filter out addresses for our second route map.

Portland(config)#access-list 101 permit ip 192.168.1.0 0.0.0.255 172.16.1.0 0.0.0.255	Creates an extended ACL, resulting in a filter based on both source and destination IP address.
Portland(config)#access-list 102 permit ip 172.16.1.0 0.0.0.255 192.168.1.0 0.0.0.255	Creates an extended ACL, resulting in a filter based on both source and destination IP address.
Portland(config)#route-map ISP1 permit 10	Creates a route map called ISP1. This route map will permit traffic based on subsequent criteria. A sequence number of 10 is assigned.
Portland(config-route-map)#match ip address 1	Specifies the match criteria— match addresses filtered from ACL 1.
Portland(config-route-map)#set interface serial 0/0/0	Specifies the set actions (what action is to be performed if the match criterion is met); in this case, forward packets out interface serial 0/0/0.
Portland(config-route-map)#exit	Returns to global configuration mode.
Portland(config)#route-map ISP2 permit 10	Creates a route map called ISP2.
Portland(config-route-map)#match ip address 2	Specifies the match criteria— match addresses filtered from ACL 2.
Portland(config-route-map)#set interface serial 0/0/1	Specifies the set actions (what action is to be performed if the match criterion is met); in this case, forward packets out interface serial 0/0/1.
Portland(config-route-map)#exit	Returns to global configuration mode.
Portland(config)#route-map 192To172 permit 10	Creates a route map named 192To172. This route map will permit traffic based on subsequent criteria. A sequence number of 10 is assigned.

Portland(config-route-map)#**match ip address 101**	Specifies the match criteria— match addresses filtered from ACL 101.
Portland(config-route-map)#**set interface fastethernet 0/1**	Specifies the set actions—forward packets out interface FastEthernet 0/1.
Portland(config-route-map)#**exit**	Returns to global configuration mode.
Portland(config)#**route-map 172To192 permit 10**	Creates a route map named 172To192.
Portland(config-route-map)#**match ip address 102**	Specifies the match criteria— match addresses filtered from ACL 102.
Portland(config-route-map)#**set interface fastethernet 0/0**	Specifies the set actions—forward packets out interface FastEthernet 0/0.
Portland(config-route-map)#**exit**	Returns to global configuration mode.
Portland(config)#**interface serial 0/0/0**	Moves to interface configuration mode.
Portland(config-if)#**description link to ISP1**	Sets a locally significant description of the interface.
Portland(config-if)#**ip address 198.133.219.1 255.255.255.252**	Assigns an IP address and netmask.
Portland(config-if)#**no shutdown**	Enables the interface.
Portland(config)#**interface serial 0/0/1**	Moves to interface configuration mode.
Portland(config-if)#**description link to ISP2**	Sets a locally significant description of the interface.
Portland(config-if)#**ip address 192.31.7.1 255.255.255.252**	Assigns an IP address and netmask.
Portland(config-if)#**no shutdown**	Enables the interface.
Portland(config)#**interface fastethernet 0/0**	Moves to interface configuration mode.

Portland(config-if)#ip address 192.168.1.1 255.255.255.0	Configures an IP address and netmask.
Portland(config-if)#ip policy route-map ISP1	Applies the route map named ISP1 to this interface.
Portland(config-if)#ip policy route-map 192To172	Applies the route map named 192To172 to this interface.
Portland(config-if)#no shutdown	Enables the interface.
Portland(config-if)#exit	Returns to global configuration mode.
Portland(config)#interface fastethernet 0/1	Moves to interface configuration mode.
Portland(config-if)#ip address 172.16.1.1 255.255.255.0	Configures an IP address and netmask.
Portland(config-if)#ip policy route-map ISP2	Applies the route map named ISP2 to this interface.
Portland(config-if)#ip policy route-map 172To192	Applies the route map named 172To192 to this interface.
Portland(config-if)#no shutdown	Enables the interface.
Portland(config-if)#exit	Returns to global configuration mode.
Portland(config)#exit	Returns to privileged mode.
Portland#copy running-config startup-config	Saves the configuration to NVRAM.

Passive Interfaces

Router(config)#router rip	Starts the RIP routing process.
Router(config-router)#passive-interface serial 0/0/0	Sets the interface as passive—meaning routing updates will not be sent out this interface.
	NOTE: For RIP, the passive-interface command will prevent the interface from sending out routing updates but will allow the interface to receive updates.

Router(config)#**router rip**	Starts the RIP routing process.
Router(config-router)#**passive-interface default**	Sets all interfaces as passive.
	TIP: The **passive-interface default** command is useful for ISP and large enterprise networks where a distribution router may have as many as 200 interfaces.
Router(config-router)#**no passive-interface fastethernet 0/0**	Activates the Fast Ethernet interface to send and receive updates.

CAUTION: When the **passive-interface** command is used with OSPF, routing information is not sent or received through that interface. This prevents routers from becoming neighbors on that interface. A better way to control OSPF routing updates is to create a stub area, a totally stubby area, or a not-so-stubby area (NSSA).

CAUTION: When the **passive-interface** command is used with EIGRP, inbound and outbound Hello packets are prevented from being sent. This will not allow EIGRP neighbors to be created. A passive interface cannot send EIGRP Hellos, which prevents adjacency relationships with link partners. An administrator can create a "pseudo" passive EIGRP interface by using a route filter that suppresses all routes from the EIGRP routing update. An example of this is shown in Chapter 2, "Implementing an EIGRP-based Solution."

Route Redistribution

Cisco routers support up to 30 dynamic routing processes. These can be different protocols—such as Open Shortest Path First (OSPF), Enhanced Interior Gateway Protocol (EIGRP), Intermediate System-to-Intermediate System (IS-IS), Routing Information Protocol (RIP), and so on—or the same protocol, but multiple processes of it, such as EIGRP 10 and EIGRP 15. Multiple instances of the same routing protocol are not recommended.

To support multiple routing protocols within the same internetwork efficiently, routing information must be shared among the different protocols. For example, routes learned from an OSPF process might need to be imported into an EIGRP process.

The process of exchanging routing information between routing protocols is called *route redistribution.*

Assigning Metrics

`Router(config)#router rip`	Starts the RIP routing process.
`Router(config-router)#redistribute eigrp 10 metric 3`	Redistributes routes learned from EIGRP autonomous system 10. The **metric** keyword assigns a starting metric of 3 for RIP—in the case of RIP, 3 hops.
`Router(config-router)#default-metric 3`	Assigns a starting metric of 3 for all routes being redistributed into RIP.

NOTE: If both the **metric** keyword in the **redistribute** command and the **default-metric** command are used, the value of the **metric** keyword in the **redistribute** command takes precedence.

TIP: If a value is not specified for the **metric** option, and no value is specified using the **default-metric** command, the default metric value is 0, except for OSPF, where the default cost is 20. Zero is only understood by IS-IS and not by RIP or EIGRP. RIP and EIGRP must have the appropriate metrics assigned to any redistributed routes; otherwise, redistribution will not work.

TIP: In the **redistribution** command, use a value for the **metric** argument that is consistent with the destination protocol.

TIP: The **default-metric** command is useful when routes are being redistributed from more than one source because it eliminates the need for defining the metrics separately for each redistribution.

Redistributing Subnets

`Router(config)#router ospf 1`	Starts the OSPF routing process.
`Router(config-router)#redistribute eigrp 10 metric 100 subnets`	Redistributes routes learned from EIGRP autonomous system 10. A metric of 100 is assigned to all routes. Subnets will also be redistributed.
	NOTE: Without the **subnets** command, only the classful address would be redistributed.
`Router(config)#router ospf 1`	Starts the OSPF routing process.

`Router(config-router)#`**`redistribute`** **`connected`**	Redistributes all directly connected networks.
	NOTE: The **connected** keyword refers to routes that are established automatically by virtue of having enabled IP on an interface. For routing protocols such as OSPF and IS-IS, these routes will be redistributed as external to the autonomous system.
`Router(config-router)#`**`redistribute`** **`connected metric 50`**	Redistributes all directly connected networks and assigns them a starting metric of 50.
	NOTE: The **redistribute connected** command is *not* affected by the **default-metric** command.

Assigning E1 or E2 Routes in OSPF

`Router(config)#`**`router ospf 1`**	Starts the OSPF routing process.
`Router(config-router)#`**`redistribute`** **`eigrp 1 metric-type 1`**	Redistributes routes learned from EIGRP autonomous system 1. Routes will be advertised as E1 routes.
	NOTE: If the **metric-type** argument is not used, routes will be advertised in OSPF as E2 routes. E2 routes have a fixed cost associated with them. The metric will not change as the route is propagated throughout the OSPF area. E1 routes will have internal area costs added to the seed metric.

Defining Seed Metrics

`Router(config)#`**`router eigrp 100`**	Starts the EIGRP routing process.
`Router(config-router)#`**`redistribute`** **`ospf 1 metric 10000 100 255 1 1500`**	Redistributes routes learned from OSPF process 1. The metrics assigned to these routes will be as follows: 10000 = Bandwidth in kbps 100 = Delay in microseconds 255 = Reliability out of 255 1 = Load out of 255 1500 = Maximum transmission unit (MTU) size

NOTE: The values used in this command constitute the *seed metric* for these routes. The seed metric is the initial value of an imported route.

NOTE: The default seed metrics for each protocol are as follows:
- Protocol: Default seed metric
- RIP: Infinity
- EIGRP: Infinity
- OSPF: 20 for all except for BGP, which is 1
- BGP: BGP metric is set to IGP metric value

NOTE: RIP and EIGRP must have the appropriate metrics assigned to any redistributed routes; otherwise, redistribution will not work.

TIP: Redistributed routes between EIGRP processes do not need metrics configured. Redistributed routes are tagged as EIGRP external routes and will appear in the routing table with a code of D EX.

Redistributing Static Routes

`Router(config)#`**`router ospf 1`**	Starts the OSPF routing process.
`Router(config-router)#`**`redistribute static`**	Redistributes static routes on this router into the OSPF routing process.

Redistributing OSPF Internal and External Routes

`Router(config)#`**`router eigrp 10`**	Starts the EIGRP routing process for autonomous system 10.
`Router(config-router)#`**`redistribute ospf 1 match internal external 1 external 2`**	Redistributes routes learned from OSPF process ID 1. The keywords **match internal external 1** and **external 2** instruct EIGRP to redistribute internal OSPF routes (and external Type 1 and Type 2 routes).
	NOTE: The default behavior when redistributing OSPF routes is to redistribute all routes—internal, external 1, and external 2. The keywords **match internal external 1** and **external 2** are required only if router behavior is to be modified.

Using Route Maps with Route Redistribution and Route Tags to Prevent Routing Loops

Figure 4-4 shows a network topology that displays a potential for routing loops. Simple two-way route redistribution could result in a loop after a route is lost from the routing table.

Figure 4-4   *Network Topology Showing Potential Loops After Two-way Redistribution*

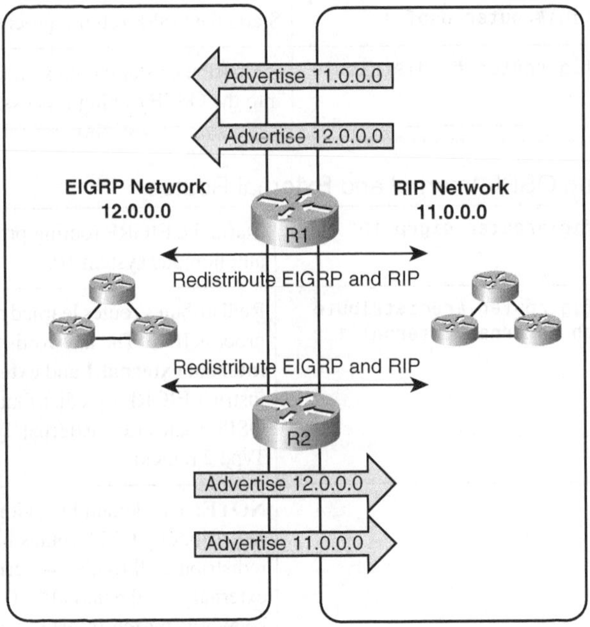

Simple two-way redistribution would be configured as follows (done on both R1 and R2):

R*x*(config)#**router rip**	Enables RIP routing process.
R*x*(config-router)#**network 11.0.0.0**	Advertises network 11.0.0.0.
R*x*(config-router)#**redistribute eigrp 40 metric 3**	Redistributes routes from EIGRP 40 into RIP and assigns a metric (hop count) of 3 to all routes.
R*x*(config-router)#**exit**	Returns to global configuration mode.
R*x*(config)#**router eigrp 40**	Enables EIGRP routing process with an autonomous system number of 40.
R*x*(config-router)#**network 12.0.0.0**	Advertises network 12.0.0.0.
R*x*(config-router)#**redistribute rip metric 10000 100 255 1 1500**	Redistributes routes from RIP into EIGRP 40 and assigns a default metric to these routes.
R*x*(config-router)#**exit**	Returns to global configuration mode.

To prevent routing loops, use route maps with route tagging.

Figure 4-5 shows a network topology that offers a solution using route tagging.

Figure 4-5   Network Topology Showing Solution to Routing Loops Using Route Tagging

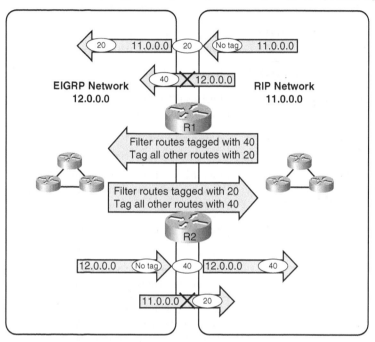

The following configuration needs to be entered into both routers—R1 and R2:

Rx(config)#**router rip**	Enables RIP routing process.
Rx(config-router)#**network 11.0.0.0**	Advertises network 11.0.0.0.
Rx(config-router)#**redistribute eigrp 40 route-map INTORIP**	Redistributes routes from EIGRP 40 into RIP and applies a route map named INTORIP to these routes.
Rx(config-router)#**exit**	Returns to global configuration mode.
Rx(config)#**route-map INTORIP deny 10**	Creates a route map called INTORIP. This route map will deny traffic based on subsequent criteria. A sequence number of 10 is assigned.
Rx(config-route-map)#**match tag 20**	Any route with a tag of 20 (a route from RIP being redistributed into EIGRP) assigned to it will be denied from being redistributed into RIP.

R*x*(config-route-map)#**exit**	Returns to global configuration mode.
R*x*(config)#**route-map INTORIP permit 20**	Creates a route map called INTORIP. This route map will permit traffic based on subsequent criteria. A sequence number of 20 is assigned.
R*x*(config-route-map)#**set tag 40**	Assigns a tag of 40 to any route from EIGRP that is being redistributed into RIP.
R*x*(config-route-map)#**exit**	Returns to global configuration mode.
R*x*(config)#**router eigrp 40**	Enables EIGRP routing process with an autonomous system number of 40.
R*x*(config-router)#**network 12.0.0.0**	Advertises network 12.0.0.0.
R*x*(config-router)#**redistribute rip route-map INTOEIGRP**	Redistributes routes from RIP into EIGRP and applies a route map named INTOEIGRP to these routes.
R*x*(config-router)#**exit**	Returns to global configuration mode.
R*x*(config)#**route-map INTOEIGRP deny 10**	Creates a route map called INTOEIGRP. This route map will deny traffic based on subsequent criteria. A sequence number of 10 is assigned.
R*x*(config-route-map)#**match tag 40**	Any route with a tag of 40 assigned to it (a route from EIGRP being redistributed into RIP) will be denied from being redistributed into EIGRP.
R*x*(config-route-map)#**exit**	Returns to global configuration mode.
R*x*(config)#**route-map INTOEIGRP permit 20**	Creates a route map called INTOEIGRP. This route map will permit traffic based on subsequent criteria. A sequence number of 20 is assigned.
R*x*(config-route-map)#**set tag 20**	Assigns a tag of 20 to any route from RIP that is being redistributed into EIGRP.
R*x*(config-route-map)#**exit**	Returns to global configuration mode.
R*x*(config)#	In global configuration mode.

Verifying Route Redistribution

`Router#`**`show ip route`**	Displays the current state of the routing table.
`Router#`**`show ip eigrp`** **`topology`**	Displays the EIGRP topology table.
`Router#`**`show ip protocols`**	Displays parameters and the current state of any active routing process.
`Router#`**`show ip rip database`**	Displays summary address entries in the RIP routing database.

Administrative Distances

The Cisco default administrative distances (AD) are as follows:

Route Source	AD
Connected interface	0
Static route	1
EIGRP summary route	5
External Border Gateway Protocol (BGP)	20
EIGRP	90
Interior Gateway Routing Protocol (IGRP)	100
OSPF	110
IS-IS	115
RIP	120
Exterior Gateway Protocol (EGP)	140
External EIGRP	170
Internal BGP	200
Unknown	255

The commands to change the administrative distance of a route from its default setting are
as follows:

Router(config)#**router ospf 1**	Starts the OSPF routing process.
Router(config-router)#**distance 95**	Changes the AD of OSPF from 110 to 95.
Router(config-router)#**distance 105 192.168.10.2 0.0.0.0**	Applies an AD of 105 to all OSPF routes received from 192.169.10.2.
	NOTE: This newly assigned AD is locally significant only. All other routers will still apply an AD of 110 to these routes.
Router(config)#**router ospf 1**	Starts the OSPF routing process.
Router(config-router)#**distance 105 172.16.10.2 0.0.0.0**	Applies an AD of 105 to all OSPF routes received from 172.16.10.2.
Router(config-router)#**distance 95 172.16.20.2 0.0.0.0 2**	Assigns an AD of 95 to any routes matching ACL 2 that are learned from 172.16.20.2.
Router(config-router)#**exit**	Returns to global configuration mode.
Router(config)#**access-list 2 permit 192.168.30.0 0.0.0.255**	Creates an ACL that will define what route or routes will have an AD of 95 assigned to it.
	NOTE: A named ACL can also be used. Replace the ACL number with the name of the ACL in this command: Router(config-router)#**distance 95 172.16.20.2 255.255.255.0 namedACL**

Static Routes: permanent Keyword

Router(config)#**ip route 192.168.50.0 255.255.255.0 serial 0/0/0 permanent**	Creates a static route that will not be removed from the routing table, even if the interface shuts down for any reason.

TIP: Without the **permanent** keyword in a static route statement, a static route will be removed if an interface goes down. A downed interface will cause the directly connected network and any associated static routes to be removed from the routing table. If the interface comes back up, the routes will be returned.

Adding the **permanent** keyword to a static route statement will keep the static routes in the routing table even if the interface goes down and the directly connected networks are removed. You *cannot* get to these routes—the interface is down—but the routes remain in the table. The advantage to this is that when the interface comes back up, the static routes do not need to be reprocessed and placed back into the routing table, saving time and processing power.

When a static route is added or deleted, this route, along with all other static routes, is processed in one second. Before Cisco IOS Release 12.0, this was 5 seconds.

The routing table processes static routes every minute to install or remove static routes according to the changing routing table.

Floating Static Routes

`Router(config)#ip route 192.168.50.0` `255.255.255.0 serial 0/0/0 130`	Creates a static route that has an AD of 130 rather than the default AD of 1.

TIP: By default, a static route will always be used rather than a routing protocol. By adding an AD number to your **ip route** statement, you can effectively create a backup route to your routing protocol. If your network is using EIGRP, and you need a backup route, add a static route with an AD greater than 90. EIGRP will be used because its AD is better (lower) than the static route. If EIGRP goes down, the static route is used in its place. When EIGRP is running again, EIGRP routes are used because their AD will again be lower than the AD of the floating static route.

Static Routes and Recursive Lookups

A static route that uses a next-hop address (intermediate address) will cause the router to look at the routing table twice: once when a packet first enters the router and the router looks up the entry in the table, and a second time when the router has to resolve the location of the intermediate address.

For point-to-point links, always use an exit interface in your static route statements:

`Router(config)#ip route 192.168.10.0 255.255.255.0 serial 0/0/0`

For broadcast links such as Ethernet or Fast Ethernet, use *both* an exit interface and intermediate address:

`Router(config)#ip route 192.168.10.0 255.255.255.0 fastethernet 0/0`
`192.138.20.2`

This saves the router from having to do a recursive lookup for the intermediate address of 192.168.20.2, knowing that the exit interface is FastEthernet 0/0.

Try to avoid using static routes that reference only intermediate addresses.

CHAPTER 5

Implementing Path Control

This chapter provides information concerning the following topics related to implementing path control:

- Offset lists
- Cisco IOS IP Service Level Agreements
- Policy routing using route maps
- Configuration example: route maps

> **NOTE:** Path control is the mechanism that changes default packet forwarding across a network. It is not quality of service (QoS) or MPLS Traffic Engineering (MPLS-TE). Path control is a collection of tools or a set of commands that is able to manipulate the routing protocol forwarding table or to bypass default packet forwarding. The manipulation of routing information may be required to obtain better resiliency, performance, or availability in your network.
>
> There are other filters or tools available to assist in the manipulation of the routing table. These include
>
> - Route maps
> - Prefix lists
> - Distribute lists
> - Administrative distance
> - Route tagging
>
> These are mostly protocol dependent and have been covered in other chapters in this book.

Offset Lists

> **NOTE:** The **offset-list** command is only applicable to EIGRP and RIP routing protocols. The **offset-list** command is used to add an offset to incoming and outgoing metrics to routes learned using these protocols. The offset value is added to the metric.

TIP: An offset list with an interface type and number is considered to be extended and will take precedence over an offset list that is not extended. This means that if an entry passes the extended offset list and the normal offset list, the offset of the extended offset list is added to the metric.

`Router(config)#router eigrp 11`	Enables EIGRP routing process with an autonomous system number of 11.
`Router(config-router)#offset-list 21 out 10`	Applies an offset list of 10 to the delay component (outgoing metrics) of a router to networks matching ACL 21.
`Router(config-router)#offset-list 21 in 10 fastethernet 0/0`	Applies an offset list of 10 to the incoming metrics of routes matching ACL 21 learned from interface FastEthernet 0/0.

Cisco IOS IP Service Level Agreements

NOTE: Cisco IOS IP Service Level Agreements (SLAs) are used to perform network performance measurements within Cisco Systems devices using active traffic monitoring.

TIP: SLAs use timestamp information to calculate performance metrics such as jitter, latency, network and server response times, packet loss, and mean opinion score.

Figure 5-1 shows the network topology for the configuration that follows, which shows the use of Cisco IOS IP SLA functionality for path control.

Figure 5-1   Cisco IOS IP Service Level Agreements

Customer requirements:

- Customer A is multihoming to ISP-1 and ISP-2.
- The link to ISP-1 is the primary link for all traffic.
- Customer A is using default routes to the ISPs instead of BGP.
- Customer A is using static routes with different administrative distances to make ISP-1 the preferred route.

Potential problem: If ISP-1 is having uplink connectivity problems to the Internet, Customer A will still be sending all of its traffic to ISP-1, only to have that traffic lost.

Solution: IOS IP SLA will be used to announce conditionally the default route to ensure reachability of a specific destination.

Follow these steps to configure Cisco IOS IP SLA functionality:

Step 1.   Define one (or more) probes.

Step 2.   Define one (or more) tracking objects.

Step 3.   Define the action on the tracking object(s).

Step 4.   Verify IP SLA operations.

Step 1: Define One (or More) Probes

`R1(config)#ip sla monitor 22`	Begins configuration for an IP SLA operation and enters SLA monitor configuration mode. 22 is the operation number and is a number between 1–2147483647.
`R1(config-sla-monitor)#type echo protocol ipIcmpEcho 10.1.1.1 source-interface fastethernet 0/0`	Defines an ICMP Echo operation to destination address 10.1.1.1 through source interface of FastEthernet 0/0 and enters ICMP Echo configuration mode.
`R1(config-sla-monitor-echo)#frequency 10`	Sets the rate at which the operation repeats. Measured in seconds from 1–604800 (7 days).
`R1(config-sla-monitor-echo)#exit`	Exits IP SLA Monitor ICMP Echo configuration mode and returns to global configuration mode.
`R1(config)#ip sla monitor schedule 22 life forever start-time now`	Sets a schedule for IP SLA monitor 22. Packets will be sent out immediately and will continue forever.

Step 2: Define One (or More) Tracking Objects

`R1(config)#track 1 sla 22 reachability`	Configures the tracking process to track the reachability of IP SLAs operation 22.
	NOTE: This command was introduced in Cisco IOS Release 12.4(20)T and replaces the **track rtr** command.

Step 3: Define the Action on the Tracking Object(s)

`R1(config)#ip route 0.0.0.0 0.0.0.0` `11.1.1.1 3 track 1`	Announces a default route to 11.1.1.1 with an administrative distance of 3 if the tracking object 1 is true.

Step 4: Verify IP SLA Operations

`R1#show ip sla configuration`	Displays SLA components such as frequency, target address, scheduling, and other parameters.
`R1#show ip sla statistics 22`	Displays number of successful and failed probes, last operation, start time, and last return code for SLA monitor 22.
`R1#show ip sla statistics 22 detail`	Displays more in-depth output for SLA monitor 22.

Policy Routing Using Route Maps

`Router(config)#`**`route-map ISP1`** **`permit 20`**	Creates a route map named ISP1. This route map will permit traffic based on subsequent criteria. A sequence number of 20 is assigned.
	NOTE: In route maps, the default action is to permit.
	NOTE: The *sequence-number* is used to indicate what position the route map is to have in a list of route maps configured with the same name.
	If no sequence number is given, the first condition in the route map is automatically numbered as 10.
`Router(config-route-map)#`**`match ip`** **`address 1`**	Specifies the match criteria (the conditions that should be tested); in this case, match addresses filtered using ACL 1.
`Router(config-route-map)#`**`set ip`** **`next hop 6.6.6.6`**	Specifies that packets that pass a match are output to the router at IP address 6.6.6.6.
`Router(config-route-map)#`**`set`** **`interface serial 0/0/0`**	Specifies the set actions (what action is to be performed if the match criteria is met); in this case, forward packets out interface serial 0/0/0.
	NOTE: If no explicit route exists in the routing table for the destination network address of the packet (that is, the packet is a broadcast packet or destined to an unknown address), the **set interface** command has no effect and is ignored.
	NOTE: A default route in the routing table will not be considered an explicit route for an unknown destination address.

`Router(config-route-map)#set ip default next hop 6.6.6.6`	Defines where to output packets that pass a match clause of a route map for policy routing and for which the Cisco IOS software has no explicit route to a destination.
`Router(config-route-map)#set default interface serial 0/0/0`	Defines where to output packets that pass a match clause of a route map for policy routing and have no explicit route to the destination.
	NOTE: This is recommended for point-to-point links only.
`Router(config-route-map)#exit`	Returns to global configuration mode.
`Router(config)#interface fastethernet 0/0`	Moves to interface configuration mode.
`Router(config-if)#ip policy route-map ISP1`	Specifies a route map to use for policy routing on an incoming interface that is receiving the packets that need to be policy routed.
`Router(config-if)#exit`	Returns to global configuration mode.
`Router(config)#ip local policy route-map ISP1`	Specifies a route map to use for policy routing on all packets originating on the router.

TIP: Packets that are generated by the router are not normally policy routed. Using the **ip local policy route-map** [*map-name*] command will make these packets adhere to a policy. For example, you may want packets originating at the router to take a route other than the obvious shortest path.

`Router(config)#interface fastethernet 0/0`	Moves to interface configuration mode.
`Router(config-if)#ip route-cache policy`	Enables fast-switched policy routing.

NOTE: Policy-based routing (PBR) must be configured before PBR fast switching can be enabled. Fast switching of PBR is disabled by default. CEF-switched PBR is enabled by default.

A fast-switched PBR supports all the **match** commands and most of the **set** commands except for the following:

- The **set ip default next-hop** command is not supported.
- The **set interface** command is supported over point-to-point links, unless a route cache entry exists that uses the same interface that is specified in the **set interface** command in the route map.

NOTE: The **ip route-cache policy** command is strictly for fast-switched PBR, and therefore not required for a CEF-switched PBR.

Router#**show ip policy**	Displays route maps that are configured on the interfaces.
Router#**show route-map** [*map-name*]	Displays route maps.
Router#**debug ip policy**	Enables the display of IP policy routing events.
Router#**traceroute**	Enables the extended **traceroute** command, which allows the specification of the source address.
Router#**ping**	Enables the extended **ping** command, which allows for the specification of the source address.

Configuration Example: Route Maps

Figure 5-2 shows the network topology for the configuration that follows, which demonstrates how to configure route maps using the commands covered in this chapter.

Figure 5-2   Network Topology for Route Map Configuration

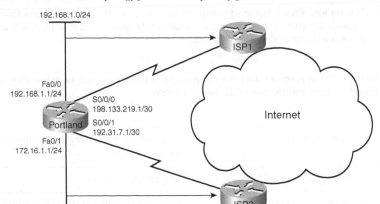

Assume for this example that you want to enforce the following policy:

- Internet-bound traffic from 192.168.1.0/24 is to be routed to ISP1.
- Internet-bound traffic from 172.16.1.0/24 is to be routed to ISP2.
- All other traffic to be routed normally according to their destination addresses.

Portland Router

Router>`enable`	Moves to privileged mode.
Router#`configure terminal`	Moves to global configuration mode.
Router(config)#`hostname Portland`	Sets the hostname of this router.
Portland(config)#`access-list 1 permit 192.168.1.0 0.0.0.255`	Creates ACL 1, which will filter out addresses for our first route map.
Portland(config)#`access-list 2 permit 172.16.1.0 0.0.0.255`	Creates ACL 2, which will filter out addresses for our second route map.
Portland(config)#`access-list 101 permit ip 192.168.1.0 0.0.0.255 172.16.1.0 0.0.0.255`	Creates an extended ACL, resulting in a filter based on both source and destination IP address.

Portland(config)#**access-list 102 permit ip 172.16.1.0 0.0.0.255 192.168.1.0 0.0.0.255**	Creates an extended ACL, resulting in a filter based on both source and destination IP address.
Portland(config)#**route-map ISP1 permit 10**	Creates a route map called ISP1. This route map will permit traffic based on subsequent criteria. A sequence number of 10 is assigned.
Portland(config-route-map)#**match ip address 1**	Specifies the match criteria—match addresses filtered from ACL 1.
Portland(config-route-map)#**set interface serial 0/0/0**	Specifies the set actions (what action is to be performed if the match criteria is met); in this case, forward packets out interface s0/0.
Portland(config-route-map)#**exit**	Returns to global configuration mode.
Portland(config)#**route-map ISP2 permit 10**	Creates a route map called ISP2.
Portland(config-route-map)#**match ip address 2**	Specifies the match criteria—match addresses filtered from ACL 2.
Portland(config-route-map)#**set interface serial 0/0/1**	Specifies the set actions (what action is to be performed if the match criteria is met); in this case, forward packets out interface s0/1.
Portland(config-route-map)#**exit**	Returns to global configuration mode.
Portland(config)#**route-map 192To172 permit 10**	Creates a route map named 192To172. This route map will permit traffic based on subsequent criteria. A sequence number of 10 is assigned.
Portland(config-route-map)#**match ip address 101**	Specifies the match criteria—match addresses filtered from ACL 101.

`Portland(config-route-map)#set interface fastethernet 0/1`	Specifies the set actions—forward packets out interface FastEthernet 0/1.
`Portland(config-route-map)#exit`	Returns to global configuration mode.
`Portland(config)#route-map 172To192 permit 10`	Creates a route map named 172To192.
`Portland(config-route-map)#match ip address 102`	Specifies the match criteria—match addresses filtered from ACL 102.
`Portland(config-route-map)#set interface fastethernet 0/0`	Specifies the set actions—forward packets out interface FastEthernet 0/0.
`Portland(config-route-map)#exit`	Returns to global configuration mode.
`Portland(config)#interface serial 0/0/0`	Moves to interface configuration mode.
`Portland(config-if)#description link to ISP1`	Sets a locally significant description of the interface.
`Portland(config-if)#ip address 198.133.219.1 255.255.255.252`	Assigns an IP address and netmask.
`Portland(config-if)#no shutdown`	Enables the interface.
`Portland(config)#interface serial 0/0/1`	Moves to interface configuration mode.
`Portland(config-if)#description link to ISP2`	Sets a locally significant description of the interface.
`Portland(config-if)#ip address 192.31.7.1 255.255.255.252`	Assigns an IP address and netmask.
`Portland(config-if)#no shutdown`	Enables the interface.
`Portland(config)#interface fastethernet 0/0`	Moves to interface configuration mode.
`Portland(config-if)#ip address 192.168.1.1 255.255.255.0`	Configures an IP address and netmask.

`Portland(config-if)#ip policy route-map ISP1`	Applies the route map named ISP1 to this interface.
`Portland(config-if)#ip policy route-map 192To172`	Applies the route map named 192To172 to this interface.
`Portland(config-if)#no shutdown`	Enables the interface.
`Portland(config-if)#exit`	Returns to global configuration mode.
`Portland(config)#interface fastethernet 0/1`	Moves to interface configuration mode.
`Portland(config-if)#ip address 172.16.1.1 255.255.255.0`	Configures an IP address and netmask.
`Portland(config-if)#ip policy route-map ISP2`	Applies the route map named ISP2 to this interface.
`Portland(config-if)#ip policy route-map 172To192`	Applies the route map named 172To192 to this interface.
`Portland(config-if)#no shutdown`	Enables the interface.
`Portland(config-if)#exit`	Returns to global configuration mode.
`Portland(config)#exit`	Returns to privileged mode.
`Portland#copy running-config startup-config`	Saves the configuration to NVRAM.

CHAPTER 6

Enterprise to ISP Connectivity

This chapter provides information and commands concerning the following enterprise to ISP connectivity topics:

- Configuring BGP
- BGP and loopback addresses
- eBGP multihop
- Verifying BGP connections
- Troubleshooting BGP connections
- Autonomous system synchronization
- Default routes
- Load balancing
- Authentication
- Attributes
  - Route selection decision process
  - Origin
  - Next hop
  - Autonomous system path: remove private autonomous system
  - Autonomous system path: prepend
  - Weight: the **weight** command
  - Weight: access lists
  - Weight: route maps
  - Local preference: the **bgp default local-preference** command
  - Local preference: route maps
  - Multi-exit discriminator (MED)
  - Atomic aggregate
- Regular expressions
- BGP route filtering using access lists
- BGP route filtering using prefix lists
- Configuration example: BGP

Configuring BGP

`Router(config)#`**`router bgp 100`**	Starts BGP routing process 100.
	NOTE: Cisco IOS software permits only one BGP process to run at a time; therefore, a router cannot belong to more than one autonomous system.
`Router(config-router)#`**`network`** **`192.135.250.0`**	Tells the BGP process what locally learned networks to advertise.
	NOTE: The networks can be connected routes, static routes, or routes learned via a dynamic routing protocol, such as Open Shortest Path First (OSPF).
	NOTE: Configuring just a **network** statement will *not* establish a BGP neighbor relationship.
	NOTE: The networks must also exist in the local router's routing table; otherwise, they will not be sent out in updates.
`Router(config-router)#`**`network`** **`128.107.0.0 mask 255.255.255.0`**	Used to specify an individual subnet.

TIP: Routes learned by the BGP process are propagated by default but are often filtered by a routing policy.

CAUTION: If you misconfigure a **network** command, such as the example **network 192.168.1.1 mask 255.255.255.0**, BGP will look for exactly 192.168.1.1/24 in the routing table. It may find 192.168.1.0/24 or 192.168.1.1/32; however, it never finds 192.168.1.1/24. Because there is no match to the network, BGP does not announce this network to any neighbors.

TIP: If you issue the command **network 192.168.0.0 mask 255.255.0.0** to advertise a CIDR block, BGP will look for 192.168.0.0/16 in the routing table. It may find 192.168.1.0/24 or 192.168.1.1/32; however, it never finds 192.168.0.0/16. Because there is no match to the network, BGP does not announce this network to any neighbors. In this case, you can configure a static route towards a null interface so BGP can find an exact match in the routing table:

```
ip route 192.168.0.0 255.255.0.0 null0
```

After finding this exact match in the routing table, BGP will announce the 192.168.0.0/16 network to any neighbors.

Router(config-router)#**neighbor 192.31.7.1 remote-as 200**	Identifies a peer router with which this router will establish a BGP session. The autonomous system number will determine whether the neighbor router is an eBGP or iBGP neighbor.
	TIP: If the autonomous system number configured in the **router bgp** command is identical to the autonomous system number configured in the **neighbor** statement, BGP initiates an internal session—iBGP. If the field values differ, BGP builds an external session—eBGP.
Router(config-router)#**neighbor 24.1.1.2 shutdown**	Disables the active session between the local router and 24.1.1.2
Router(config-router)#**no neighbor 24.1.1.2 shutdown**	Re-enables the active session between the local router and 24.1.1.2.
Router(config-router)#**timers bgp 90 240**	Changes the BGP network timers. The first number is the Keepalive timer (default, 60 seconds). The second number is the Holdtime timer (default, 180 seconds).

BGP and Loopback Addresses

Router(config)#**router bgp 100**	Starts the BGP routing process.
Router(config-router)#**neighbor 172.16.1.2 update-source loopback 0**	Informs the router to use any operational interface for TCP connections (in this case, Loopback 0). Because a loopback interface never goes down, this adds more stability to your configuration as compared to using a physical interface.
	TIP: Without the **neighbor update-source** command, BGP will use the closest IP interface to the peer. This command provides BGP with a more robust configuration, because BGP will still operate in the event the link to the closest interface fails.
	NOTE: You can use the **neighbor update-source** command with either eBGP or iBGP sessions. In the case of a point-to-point eBGP session, this command is not needed because there is only one path for BGP to use.

eBGP Multihop

Figure 6-1 shows commands necessary to configure eBGP multihop.

Figure 6-1   Network Topology for eBGP Multihop Configuration

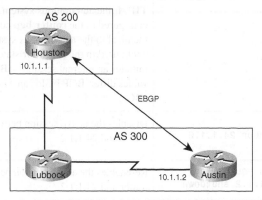

`Houston(config)#router bgp 200`	Starts the BGP routing process.
`Houston(config-router)#neighbor 10.1.1.2 remote-as 300`	Identifies a peer router at 10.1.1.2.
`Houston(config-router)#neighbor 10.1.1.2 ebgp-multihop 2`	Allows for two routers that are not directly connected to establish an eBGP session.
`Austin(config)#router bgp 300`	Starts the BGP routing process.
`Austin(config-router)#neighbor 10.1.1.1 remote-as 200`	Identifies a peer router at 10.1.1.1.
`Austin(config-router)#neighbor 10.1.1.1 ebgp-multihop 2`	Allows for two routers that are not directly connected to establish an eBGP session.

NOTE: The **ebgp-multihop** keyword is a Cisco IOS option. It must be configured on each peer. The **ebgp-multihop** keyword is only used for eBGP sessions, not for iBGP.

eBGP neighbors are usually directly connected (over a WAN connection, for example) to establish an eBGP session. However, sometimes one of the directly connected routers is unable to run BGP. The **ebgp-multihop** keyword allows for a logical connection to be made between peer routers, even if they are not directly connected. The **ebgp-multihop** keyword allows for an eBGP peer to be up to 255 hops away and still create an eBGP session.

NOTE: If redundant links exist between two eBGP neighbors and loopback addresses are used, you must configure **ebgp-multihop** because of the default TTL of 1. Otherwise, the router decrements the TTL before giving the packet to the loopback interface, meaning that the normal IP forwarding logic discards the packet.

Verifying BGP Connections

Router#`show ip bgp`	Displays entries in the BGP routing table.
Router#`show ip bgp neighbors`	Displays information about the BGP and TCP connections to neighbors.
Router#`show ip bgp rib-failure`	Displays networks that are not installed in the Routing Information Base (RIB) and the reason that they were not installed.
Router#`show ip bgp summary`	Displays the status of all BGP connections.

Troubleshooting BGP Connections

Router#`clear ip bgp *`	Forces BGP to clear its table and resets all BGP sessions.
Router#`clear ip bgp 10.1.1.1`	Resets the specific BGP session with the neighbor at 10.1.1.1.
Router#`clear ip bgp 10.1.1.2 soft out`	Forces the remote router to resend all BGP information to the neighbor without resetting the connection. Routes from this neighbor are not lost.
	TIP: The **clear ip bgp w.x.y.z soft out** command is highly recommended when you are changing an outbound policy on the router. The **soft out** option does not help if you are changing an inbound policy.
	TIP: The **soft** keyword of this command is optional; **clear ip bgp out** will do a soft reset for all outbound updates.

Router(config-router)#**neighbor 10.1.1.2 soft-reconfiguration inbound**	Causes the router to store all updates from this neighbor in case the inbound policy is changed.
	CAUTION: The **soft-reconfiguration inbound** command is memory intensive.
Router#**clear ip bgp 10.1.1.2 soft in**	Uses the stored information to generate new inbound updates.
Router#**clear ip bgp {*l10.1.1.2} [soft in l in]**	Creates a dynamic soft reset of inbound BGP routing table updates. Routes are not withdrawn. Updates are not stored locally. The connection remains established.

NOTE: Beginning with Cisco IOS Releases 12.0(2)S and 12.0(6)T, Cisco introduced a BGP soft reset enhancement feature known as *route refresh*. Route refresh is not dependent upon stored routing table update information. This method requires no preconfiguration and requires less memory than previous soft methods for inbound routing table updates.

NOTE: To determine whether a BGP router supports route refresh capability, use the **show ip bgp neighbors** command. The following message is displayed in the output when route refresh is supported:

Received route refresh capability from peer

NOTE: When a BGP session is reset and soft reconfiguration is used, there are several commands that exist to monitor BGP routes that are received, sent, or filtered:

Router#**show ip bgp**
Router#**show ip bgp neighbor address advertised**
Router#**show ip bgp neighbor address received**
Router#**show ip bgp neighbor address routes**

Router#**debug ip bgp**	Displays information related to processing BGP.

CAUTION: The **clear ip bgp** * command is both processor and memory intensive and should be used only in smaller environments. A more reasonable approach is to clear only a specific network or a specific session with a neighbor with the **clear ip bgp** *specific-network* command. However, you can use this command whenever the following changes occur:

* Additions or changes to the BGP-related access lists
* Changes to BGP-related weights
* Changes to BGP-related distribution lists
* Changes in the BGP timer's specifications
* Changes to the BGP administrative distance
* Changes to BGP-related route maps

Autonomous System Synchronization

Router(config)#**router bgp 100**	Starts the BGP routing process.
Router(config-router)#**synchronization**	Enables synchronization.

NOTE: The BGP synchronization rule states that a BGP router should not advertise to external neighbors' destinations learned from inside BGP neighbors unless those destinations are also known via an IGP.

NOTE: By default, synchronization between BGP and the IGP is turned off to allow the Cisco IOS software to advertise a network route without waiting for route validation from the IGP. This feature allows routers and access servers within an autonomous system to have the route before BGP makes it available to other autonomous systems.

TIP: Use the **synchronization** command if routers in the autonomous system do not speak BGP.

Router(config-router)#**no synchronization**	Overrides the BGP synchronization requirement.

NOTE: The **no synchronization** command is a Cisco-only command.

TIP: In two situations, you can safely turn off synchronization:
- When all transit routers inside the autonomous system are running fully meshed iBGP
- When the autonomous system is not a transit autonomous system

Default Routes

Router(config)#**router bgp 100**	Starts the BGP routing process.
Router(config-router)#**neighbor 192.168.100.1 remote-as 200**	Identifies a peer router at 192.168.100.1.
Router(config-router)#**neighbor 192.168.100.1 default-originate**	States that the default route of 0.0.0.0 will only be sent to 192.168.100.1.

NOTE: If you want your BGP router to advertise a default to all peers, use the **network** command with an address of 0.0.0.0:

RTC(config)#**router bgp 100**

RTC(config-router)#**neighbor 172.16.20.1 remote-as 150**

RTC(config-router)#**neighbor 172.17.1.1 remote-as 200**

RTC(config-router)#**network 0.0.0.0**

Load Balancing

Router(config)#**router bgp 100**	Starts the BGP routing process.
Router(config-router)#**maximum-paths 3**	Enables BGP load balancing over three equal-cost paths.
Router(config-router)#**maximum-paths ibgp 3**	Enables BGP load balancing over three equal-cost iBGP paths.
Router(config-router)#**maximum-paths eibgp 3**	Enables BGP load balancing for three equal-cost eBGP and iBGP paths.

NOTE: BGP supports a maximum of 16 paths per destination, but only if they are sourced from the same autonomous system. By default, BGP installs only one path to the IP routing table.

Authentication

Router(config)#**router bgp 100**	Starts the BGP routing process.
Router(config-router)#**neighbor 198.133.219.1 password tower**	Specifies that the router and its peer at 198.133.219.1 use Message Digest 5 (MD5) authentication on the TCP connection between them.

> **NOTE:** The password must be the same on both BGP peers. The password is case sensitive and can be up to 25 alphanumeric characters when the **service password-encryption** command is enabled, and up to 81 characters when the **service password-encryption** command is not enabled. The first character cannot be a number. The string can contain any alphanumeric characters, including spaces. You cannot specify a password in the format *number-space-anything*. The space after the number can cause authentication to fail.

Attributes

Routes learned via BGP have associated properties that are used to determine the best route to a destination when multiple paths exist to a particular destination. These properties are referred to as *BGP attributes*, and an understanding of how BGP attributes influence route selection is required for the design of robust networks. After describing the route selection process, this section will describe the attributes that BGP uses in the route selection process.

Route Selection Decision Process

The decision process for determining the best path to reach a destination is based on the following:

1   If the path specifies a next hop that is inaccessible, drop the update.

2   Prefer the path with the *largest weight*.

3   If the weights are the same, prefer the path with the *largest local preference.*

4   If the local preferences are the same, prefer the path that was *originated by BGP* running on this router.

5   If no route was originated, prefer the route that has the *shortest AS_PATH.*

6   If all paths have the same AS_PATH length, prefer the path with the *lowest origin* type (where IGP is lower than EGP, and EGP is lower than Incomplete).

7   If the origin codes are the same, prefer the path with the *lowest MED attribute.*

8   If the paths have the same MED, prefer the *external path* over the internal path.

9   If the paths are still the same, prefer the path through the *closest IGP neighbor.*

10   For eBGP paths, select the *oldest route* to minimize the effects of route flapping.

11   Prefer the route with the *lowest BGP router ID* value.

12   If the BGP router IDs are the same, prefer the router with the *lowest neighbor IP address.*

Origin

The origin attribute indicates how BGP learned about a particular route.

Router(config)#**route-map SETORIGIN permit 10**	Creates a route map called SETORIGIN. This route map will permit traffic based on subsequent criteria. A sequence number of 10 is assigned.
	NOTE: The *sequence-number* is used to indicate what position the route map is to have in a list of route map statements configured with the same name. If no sequence number is given, the first condition in the route map is automatically numbered as 10.
Router(config-route-map)#**match as-path 10**	Specifies the condition under which redistribution or policy routing is allowed. In this case, it must match routes from autonomous system path 10.
Router(config-route-map)#**set origin igp**	Sets the origin code of the routing update as IGP.
Router(config-route-map)#**exit**	Returns to global configuration mode.
Router(config)#**router bgp 100**	Starts the BGP routing process.
Router(config-router)#**redistribute eigrp 51 route-map SETORIGIN**	Redistributes EIGRP autonomous system 51 into BGP using the route map called SETORIGIN as the conditions for redistribution.

NOTE: The three options for the origin attribute in the **set origin** command are **igp**, **egp**, and **incomplete**.

Next-Hop

The eBGP next-hop attribute is the IP address that is used to reach the advertising router. For eBGP peers, the next-hop address is the IP address of the connection between the peers. For iBGP, the eBGP next-hop address is carried into the local autonomous system.

Figure 6-2 shows commands necessary to configure the next-hop attribute.

Figure 6-2   Network Topology for Next-Hop Attribute Configuration

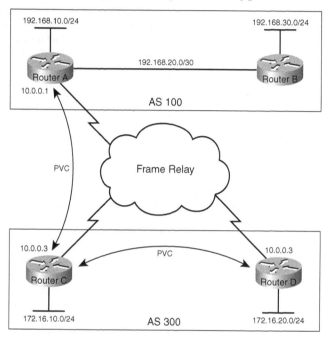

RouterC(config)#**router bgp 300**	Starts the BGP routing process.
RouterC(config-router)#**neighbor 10.0.0.1 remote-as 100**	Identifies a peer router at 10.0.0.1.
RouterC(config-router)#**neighbor 10.0.0.1 next-hop-self**	Forces all updates destined to the neighbor at 10.0.0.1 to advertise this router as the next hop.

	NOTE: Router C advertises 172.16.20.0 to Router A with a next hop of 10.0.0.3, just as it would do if the common media were Ethernet. The problem is that Router A does not have a direct permanent virtual connection (PVC) to Router D and cannot reach the next hop, so routing will fail. To remedy this situation, use the **neighbor next-hop-self** router configuration command. The **neighbor next-hop-self** command causes Router C to advertise 172.16.20.0 with the next-hop attribute set to 10.0.0.3.
	TIP: This command proves useful in nonmeshed networks (such as Frame Relay or X.25) where BGP neighbors might not have direct access to all other neighbors on the same IP subnet.
`RouterC(config-router)#neighbor 10.0.0.1 next-hop-unchanged`	Enables an eBGP multihop peer to propagate the next hop unchanged.
	CAUTION: This command should not be configured on a route reflector, and the **neighbor next-hop-self** command should not be used to modify the next-hop attribute for a route reflector when this feature is enabled for a route reflector client. Route reflectors are a solution for dealing with iBGP peering within an autonomous system. Route reflectors allow a router to advertise (reflect) iBGP-learned routes to other iBGP routers, thereby reducing the number of iBGP peers within an autonomous system.

Autonomous System Path: Remove Private Autonomous System

Private autonomous system numbers (64,512 to 65,535) cannot be passed on to the Internet because they are not unique. Cisco has implemented a feature, **remove-private-as**, to strip private autonomous system numbers out of the AS_PATH list before the routes get propagated to the Internet.

Figure 6-3 shows commands necessary to configure the **remove-private-as** option.

Figure 6-3   Network Topology for Remote Private Autonomous System Configuration

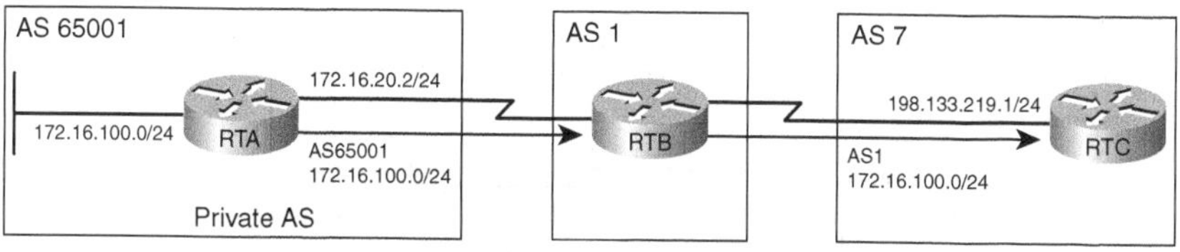

RTB(config)#router bgp 1	Starts the BGP routing process.
RTB(config-router)#neighbor 172.16.20.2 remote-as 65001	Identifies a peer router at 172.16.20.2.
RTB(config-router)#neighbor 198.133.219.1 remote-as 7	Identifies a peer router at 198.133.219.1.
RTB(config-router)#neighbor 198.133.219.1 remove-private-as	Removes private autonomous system numbers from the path in outbound routing updates.
	NOTE: The **remove-private-as** command is available for EBGP neighbors only.

Autonomous System Path: Prepend

You can influence the decision-making process with regard to the AS_PATH attribute by prepending, or adding, extra autonomous system numbers to the AS_PATH attribute. Assuming that the values of all other attributes are the same, routers will pick the shortest AS_PATH attribute; therefore, prepending numbers to the path will manipulate the decision as to the best path.

Figure 6-4 shows commands necessary to configure the **as-path prepend** option.

Figure 6-4   Network Topology for AS_PATH Prepend Configuration

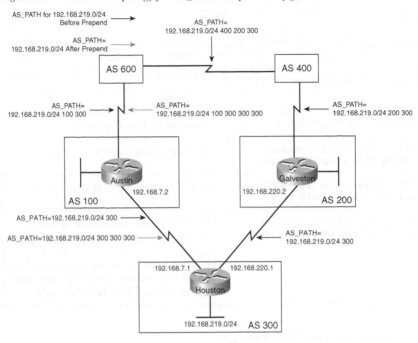

In this scenario, you want to use the configuration of Houston to influence the choice of paths in autonomous system 600. Currently, the routers in autonomous system 600 have reachability information to the 192.168.219.0/24 network via two routes: via autonomous system 100 with an AS_PATH attribute of (100, 300) and via autonomous system 400 with an AS_PATH attribute of (400, 200, 300). Assuming that the values of all other attributes are the same, the routers in autonomous system 600 will pick the shortest AS_PATH attribute: the route through autonomous system 100. You will prepend, or add, extra autonomous system numbers to the AS_PATH attribute for routes that Houston advertises to autonomous system 100 to have autonomous system 600 select autonomous system 400 as the preferred path of reaching the 192.168.219.0/24 network.

Houston(config)#**router bgp 300**	Starts the BGP routing process.
Houston(config-router)#**network 192.168.219.0**	Tells the BGP process what locally learned networks to advertise.
Houston(config-router)#**neighbor 192.168.220.2 remote-as 200**	Identifies a peer router at 192.168.220.2.
Houston(config-router)#**neighbor 192.168.7.2 remote-as 100**	Identifies a peer router at 192.168.7.2.

Houston(config-router)#**neighbor 192.168.7.2 route-map SETPATH out**	Read this command to say, "All routes destined for 192.168.7.2 will have to follow the conditions laid out by the SETPATH route map."
Houston(config-router)#**exit**	Returns to global configuration mode.
Houston(config)#**route-map SETPATH permit 10**	Creates a route map named SETPATH. This route map will permit traffic based on subsequent criteria. A sequence number of 10 is assigned.
Houston(config-route-map)#**set as-path prepend 300 300**	Read this command to say, "The local router will add (prepend) the autonomous system number 300 twice to the AS_PATH attribute before sending it out to its neighbor at 192.168.7.2."

The result of this configuration is that the AS_PATH attribute of updates for network 192.168.219.0 that autonomous system 600 receives via autonomous system 100 will be (100, 300, 300, 300), which is longer than the value of the AS_PATH attribute of updates for network 192.168.219.0 that autonomous system 600 receives via autonomous system 400 (400, 200, 300).

Autonomous system 600 will choose autonomous system 400 (400, 200, 300) as the better path. This is because BGP is a path vector routing protocol that chooses the path with the least number of autonomous systems that it has to cross.

Weight: The Weight Attribute
The weight attribute is a special Cisco attribute that is used in the path selection process when there is more than one route to the same destination.

Figure 6-5 shows commands necessary to configure the weight attribute.

Figure 6-5   Network Topology for Weight Attribute Configuration

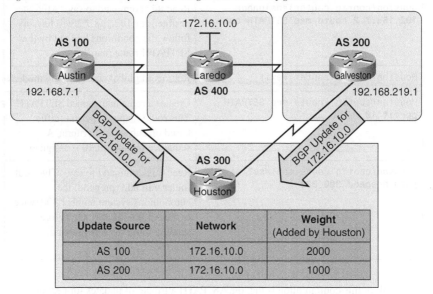

Update Source	Network	Weight (Added by Houston)
AS 100	172.16.10.0	2000
AS 200	172.16.10.0	1000

`Houston(config)#`**`router bgp 300`**	Starts the BGP routing process.
`Houston(config-router)#`**`neighbor 192.168.7.1 remote-as 100`**	Identifies a peer router at 192.168.7.1.
`Houston(config-router)#`**`neighbor 192.168.7.1 weight 2000`**	Sets the weight of all route updates from autonomous system 100 to 2000.
`Houston(config-router)#`**`neighbor 192.168.219.1 remote-as 200`**	Identifies a peer router at 192.168.219.1.
`Houston(config-router)#`**`neighbor 192.168.219.1 weight 1000`**	Sets the weight of all route updates from autonomous system 200 to 1000.

The result of this configuration will have Houston forward traffic to the 172.16.10.0 network through autonomous system 100, because the route entering autonomous system 300 from autonomous system 100 had a higher **weight** attribute set compared to that same route advertised from autonomous system 200.

> **NOTE:** The **weight** attribute is local to the router and *not propagated* to other routers. By default, the **weight** attribute is 32,768 for paths that the router originates, and 0 for other paths. Routes with a *higher weight are preferred* when there are multiple routes to the same destination.

Weight: Access Lists

Refer to Figure 6-5 to see commands necessary to configure the weight attribute using access lists.

`Houston(config)#router bgp 300`	Starts the BGP routing process.
`Houston(config-router)#neighbor 192.168.7.1 remote-as 100`	Identifies a peer router at 192.168.7.1.
`Houston(config-router)#neighbor 192.168.7.1 filter-list 5 weight 2000`	Assigns a **weight** attribute of 2000 to updates from the neighbor at 192.168.7.1 that are permitted by access list 5. Access list 5 is defined in the **ip as-path access-list 5** command listed below in global configuration mode. Filter list 5 refers to the **ip as-path access-list 5** command that defines which path will be used to have this weight value assigned to it.
`Houston(config-router)#neighbor 192.168.219.1  remote-as 200`	Identifies a peer router at 192.168.219.1.
`Houston(config-router)#neighbor 192.168.219.1 filter-list 6 weight 1000`	Assigns a **weight** attribute of 1000 to updates from the neighbor at 192.168.219.1 that are permitted by access list 6. Access list 6 is defined in the **ip as-path access-list 5** command listed below in global configuration mode.
`Houston(config-router)#exit`	Returns to global configuration mode.
`Houston(config)#ip as-path access-list 5 permit ^100$`	Permits updates whose AS_PATH attribute starts with 100 (represented by the ^) and ends with 100 (represented by the $).
	The ^ and $ symbols are used to form regular expressions. See the section "Regular Expressions" in this chapter (after the sections on the different attributes) for more examples.
`Houston(config)#ip as-path access-list 6 permit ^200$`	Permits updates whose AS_PATH attribute starts with 200 (represented by the ^) and ends with 200 (represented by the $).

The result of this configuration will have Houston forward traffic for the 172.16.10.0 network through autonomous system 100, because it has a higher weight attribute set as compared to the weight attribute set for the same update from autonomous system 200.

Weight: Route Maps

Refer to Figure 6-5 to see commands necessary to configure the weight attribute using route maps.

`Houston(config)#router bgp 300`	Starts the BGP routing process.
`Houston(config-router)#neighbor 192.168.7.1 remote-as 100`	Identifies a peer router at 192.168.7.1.
`Houston(config-router)#neighbor 192.168.7.1 route-map SETWEIGHT in`	Read this command to say, "All routes originating from 192.168.7.1 will have to follow the conditions laid out by the SETWEIGHT route map."
`Houston(config-router)#neighbor 192.168.219.1 remote-as 200`	Identifies a peer router at 192.168.219.1.
`Houston(config-router)#neighbor 192.168.219.1 route-map SETWEIGHT in`	Identifies that the route map named SETWEIGHT will be used to assign weights to route updates.
`Houston(config-router)#exit`	Returns to global configuration mode.
`Houston(config)#ip as-path access-list 5 permit ^100$`	Permits updates whose AS_PATH attribute starts with 100 (represented by the ^) and ends with 100 (represented by the $).
`Houston(config)#route-map SETWEIGHT permit 10`	Creates a route map called SETWEIGHT. This route map will permit traffic based on subsequent criteria. A sequence number of 10 is assigned.
`Houston(config-route-map)#match as-path 5`	Specifies the condition under which policy routing is allowed—matching the BGP access control list (ACL) 5.
`Houston(config-route-map)#set weight 2000`	Assigns a weight of 2000 to any route update that meets the condition of ACL 5—an AS_PATH that starts with 100 and ends with 100.

Houston(config-route-map)#exit	Returns to global configuration mode.
Houston(config)#route-map SETWEIGHT permit 20	Creates the second statement for the route map named SETWEIGHT. This route map will permit traffic based on subsequent criteria. A sequence number of 20 is assigned.
Houston(config-route-map)#set weight 1000	Assigns a weight of 1000 to route updates from any other autonomous system aside from 100—autonomous system 100 will be assigned a weight of 2000 due to the first instance of the route map.

The result of this configuration will have Houston forward traffic for the 172.16.10.0 network through autonomous system 100, because it has a higher **weight** attribute set as compared to the **weight** attribute set for the same update from autonomous system 200.

Local Preference: bgp default local-preference Command

The local preference attribute is used to indicate the preferred path to a remote destination if there are multiple paths to that destination. The local preference attribute is part of the routing update, and unlike the **weight** attribute, it will be exchanged between routers in the same autonomous system.

Figure 6-6 shows the commands necessary to configure the **bgp default local-preference** command.

Figure 6-6   *Network Topology for* **bgp default local-preference** *Configuration*

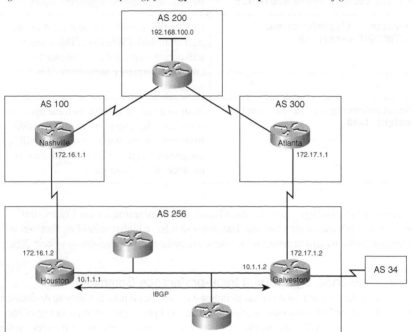

Houston(config)#**router bgp 256**	Starts the BGP routing process.
Houston(config-router)#**neighbor 172.16.1.1 remote-as 100**	Identifies a peer router at 172.16.1.1.
Houston(config-router)#**neighbor 10.1.1.2 remote-as 256**	Identifies a peer router at 10.1.1.2.
Houston(config-router)#**bgp default local-preference 150**	Sets the local preference attribute on this router.
Galveston(config)#**router bgp 256**	Starts the BGP routing process.
Galveston(config-router)#**neighbor 172.17.1.1 remote-as 300**	Identifies a peer router at 172.17.1.1.
Galveston(config-router)#**neighbor 10.1.1.1 remote-as 256**	Identifies a peer router at 10.1.1.1.
Galveston(config-router)#**bgp default local-preference 200**	Sets the local preference attribute on this router.

Based on these two configurations, traffic destined for a remote network that can be reached through autonomous system 256 will be routed through Galveston.

NOTE: The **local-preference** value can be a number between 0 and 429,496,729. Higher is preferred. If a **local-preference** value is not set, the default is 100.

NOTE: The local-preference attribute is local to the autonomous system—it is exchanged between iBGP peers but not advertised to eBGP peers. Use the local-preference attribute to force BGP routers to prefer one exit point over another.

Local Preference: Route Maps

Route maps provide more flexibility than the **bgp default local-preference** router configuration command.

Refer to Figure 6-6 to see commands necessary to configure the local-preference attribute using route maps.

Galveston(config)#**router bgp 256**	Starts the BGP routing process.
Galveston(config-router)#**neighbor 172.17.1.1 remote-as 300**	Identifies a peer router at 172.17.1.1.
Galveston(config-router)#**neighbor 172.17.1.1 route-map SETLOCAL in**	Refers to a route map called SETLOCAL.
Galveston(config-router)#**neighbor 10.1.1.1 remote-as 256**	Identifies a peer router at 10.1.1.1.
Galveston(config-router)#**exit**	Returns to global configuration mode.
Galveston(config)#**ip as-path access-list 7 permit ^300$**	Permits updates whose AS_PATH attribute starts with 300 (represented by the ^) and ends with 300 (represented by the $).
Galveston(config)#**route-map SETLOCAL permit 10**	Creates a route map called SETLOCAL. This route map will permit traffic based on subsequent criteria. A sequence number of 10 is assigned.
Galveston(config-route-map)#**match as-path 7**	Specifies the condition under which policy routing is allowed—matching the BGP ACL 7.

Galveston(config-route-map)#**set local-preference 200**	Assigns a local preference of 200 to any update coming from autonomous system 300—as defined by ACL 7.
Galveston(config-route-map)#**route-map SETLOCAL permit 20**	Creates the second statement of the route map SETLOCAL. This instance will accept all other routes.

In the previous example, using the **bgp default local-preference** command on Galveston, the local preference attribute of *all* routing updates received by Galveston would be set to 200. This would include updates from autonomous system 34. In this example, using the **route-map** command, only updates received from autonomous system 300, as specified in the **ip as_path access-list** command, will have a local preference set to 200.

Multi-Exit Discriminator (MED)

The multi-exit discriminator (MED) attribute provides a hint to external neighbors about which path to choose to an autonomous system that has multiple entry points.

Figure 6-7 shows the commands necessary to configure the MED attribute.

Figure 6-7   Network Topology for MED Attribute Configuration

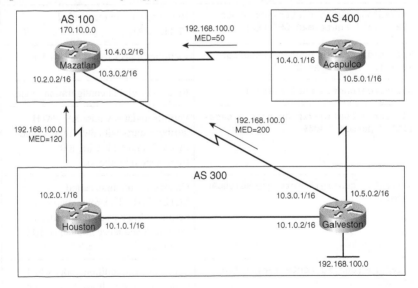

Mazatlan(config)#**router bgp 100**	Starts the BGP routing process.
Mazatlan(config-router)#**neighbor 10.2.0.1 remote-as 300**	Identifies a peer router at 10.2.0.1.
Mazatlan(config-router)#**neighbor 10.3.0.1 remote-as 300**	Identifies a peer router at 10.3.0.1.
Mazatlan(config-router)#**neighbor 10.4.0.1 remote-as 400**	Identifies a peer router at 10.4.0.1.
Acapulco(config)#**router bgp 400**	Starts the BGP routing process.
Acapulco(config-router)#**neighbor 10.4.0.2 remote-as 100**	Identifies a peer router at 10.4.0.2.
Acapulco(config-router)#**neighbor 10.4.0.2 route-map SETMEDOUT out**	Refers to a route map named SETMEDOUT.
Acapulco(config-router)#**neighbor 10.5.0.2 remote-as 300**	Identifies a peer router at 10.5.0.2.
Acapulco(config-router)#**exit**	Returns to global configuration mode.
Acapulco(config)#**route-map SETMEDOUT permit 10**	Creates a route map named SETMEDOUT. This route map will permit traffic based on subsequent criteria. A sequence number of 10 is assigned.
Acapulco(config-route-map)#**set metric 50**	Sets the metric value for BGP.
Houston(config)#**router bgp 300**	Starts the BGP routing process.
Houston(config-router)#**neighbor 10.2.0.1 remote-as 100**	Identifies a peer router at 10.2.0.1.
Houston(config-router)#**neighbor 10.2.0.1 route-map SETMEDOUT out**	Refers to a route map named SETMEDOUT.
Houston(config-router)#**neighbor 10.5.0.1 remote-as 400**	Identifies a peer router at 10.5.0.1.
Houston(config-router)#**neighbor 10.1.0.2 remote-as 300**	Identifies a peer router at 10.1.0.2.
Houston(config-router)#**exit**	Returns to global configuration mode.

`Houston(config)#`**`route-map SETMEDOUT`** **`permit 10`**	Creates a route map named SETMEDOUT. This route map will permit traffic based on subsequent criteria. A sequence number of 10 is assigned.
`Houston(config-route-map)#`**`set`** **`metric 120`**	Sets the metric value for BGP.
`Galveston(config)#`**`router bgp 300`**	Starts the BGP routing process.
`Galveston(config-router)#`**`neighbor`** **`10.3.0.2 remote-as 100`**	Identifies a peer router at 10.3.0.2.
`Galveston(config-router)#`**`neighbor`** **`10.3.0.2 route-map SETMEDOUT out`**	Refers to a route map named SETMEDOUT.
`Galveston(config-router)#`**`neighbor`** **`10.1.0.1 remote-as 300`**	Identifies a peer router at 10.1.0.1.
`Galveston(config-router)#`**`exit`**	Returns to global configuration mode.
`Galveston(config)#`**`route-map`** **`SETMEDOUT permit 10`**	Creates a route map named SETMEDOUT. This route map will permit traffic based on subsequent criteria. A sequence number of 10 is assigned.
`Galveston(config-route-map)#`**`set`** **`metric 200`**	Sets the metric value for BGP.

- A lower MED value is preferred over a higher MED value. The default value of the MED is 0.
- Unlike local preference, the MED attribute is exchanged between autonomous systems, but an MED attribute that comes into an autonomous system does not leave the autonomous system.
- Unless otherwise specified, the router compares MED attributes for paths from external neighbors that are in the same autonomous system.
- If you want MED attributes from neighbors in other autonomous systems to be compared, you must configure the **bgp always-compare-med** command.

NOTE: By default, BGP compares the MED attributes of routes coming from neighbors in the same external autonomous system *as the route* (such as autonomous system 300). Mazatlan can only compare the MED attribute coming from Houston (120) to the MED attribute coming from Galveston (200) even though the update coming from Acapulco has the lowest MED value. Mazatlan will choose Houston as the best path for reaching network 192.168.100.0.

To force Mazatlan to include updates for network 192.168.100.0 from Acapulco in the comparison, use the **bgp always-compare-med** router configuration command on Mazatlan:

```
Mazatlan(config)#router bgp 100
Mazatlan(config-router)#neighbor 10.2.0.1 remote-as 300
Mazatlan(config-router)#neighbor 10.3.0.1 remote-as 300
Mazatlan(config-router)#neighbor 10.4.0.1 remote-as 400
Mazatlan(config-router)#bgp always-compare-med
```

Mazatlan will choose Acapulco as the best next hop for reaching network 192.168.100.0 assuming that all other attributes are the same.

Atomic Aggregate

A BGP router can transmit overlapping routes (nonidentical routes that point to the same destination) to another BGP router. When making a best path decision, a router always chooses the more specific path.

Figure 6-8 shows the commands necessary to configure the atomic aggregate attribute.

Figure 6-8   Network Topology for Atomic Aggregate Attribute Configuration

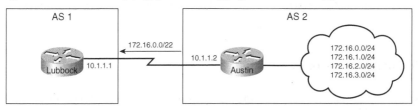

`Lubbock(config)#router bgp 1`	Starts the BGP routing process.
`Lubbock(config-router)#neighbor 10.1.1.2 remote-as 2`	Identifies a peer router at 10.1.1.2.
`Austin(config)#router bgp 2`	Starts the BGP routing process.
`Austin(config-router)#neighbor 10.1.1.1 remote-as 1`	Identifies a peer router at 10.1.1.1.
`Austin(config-router)#network 172.16.0.0 mask 255.255.255.0`	Advertises a specific subnet.
`Austin(config-router)#network 172.16.1.0 mask 255.255.255.0`	Advertises a specific subnet.
`Austin(config-router)#network 172.16.2.0 mask 255.255.255.0`	Advertises a specific subnet.

`Austin(config-router)#network` `172.16.3.0 mask 255.255.255.0`	Advertises a specific subnet.
`Austin(config-router)#aggregate-` `address 172.16.0.0 255.255.252.0`	Advertises the aggregate address.
	NOTE: To send the aggregate address, we only need one of the more specific routes configured. But by configuring all of them, the aggregate will be sent in case one of the networks goes down.

With this configuration, both Lubbock and Austin will have all the specific routes *and* the aggregate address in its BGP table—verify with **show ip bgp**:

```
Lubbock#show ip bgp 172.16.0.0 255.255.252.0
BGP routing table entry for 172.16.0.0/22, version 18
Paths: (1 available, best #1)
<text omitted>
  Origin IGP, localpref 100, valid, external, atomic-aggregate,
  best
```

Regular Expressions

A *regular expression* is a pattern to match against an input string, such as those listed in the following table.

Character	Description
^	Matches the beginning of the input string.
$	Matches the end of the input string.
_	Matches a space, comma, left brace, right brace, the beginning of an input string, or the ending of an input stream.
.	Matches any single character.
*	Matches 0 or more single- or multiple-character patterns.

For example, in the case of the **ip as-path access-list** command, the input string is the AS_PATH attribute.

`Router(config)#ip as-path access-list 1 permit 2150`	Will match any AS_PATH that includes the pattern of 2150.
`Router#show ip bgp regexp 2150`	Will match any AS_PATH that includes the pattern of 2150.
	NOTE: In both of these commands, not only will autonomous system 2150 be a match, but so will autonomous system 12150 or 21507.
`Router(config)#ip as-path access-list 6 deny ^200$`	Denies updates whose AS_PATH attribute starts with 200 (represented by the ^) and ends with 200 (represented by the $).
`Router(config)#ip as-path access-list 1 permit .*`	Permits updates whose AS_PATH attribute starts with any character (represented by the period [.] symbol). Repeats that character—the asterisk (*) symbol means a repetition of that character.
	NOTE: The argument of .* will match any value of the AS_PATH attribute.

Regular Expressions: Example One

Use the following output of the **show ip bgp** command to see how different examples of regular expressions can help filter specific patterns.

```
Router#show ip bgp
   Network        Next Hop         Metric  LocPrf  Weight  Path
*> 10.0.0.0       0.0.0.0               0           32768   i
*> 172.16.0.0     200.200.200.65        0     300     200   i
*> 192.168.2.0    200.200.200.65        0       0     300   i
Router#show ip bgp regexp ^300
```

- Match beginning of input string, AS_PATH, = 300.
- Last prepended autonomous system was 300.
- Routes matched: 172.16.0.0 and 192.168.20.0.

```
Router#show ip bgp regexp 300$
```

- Match end of input string, AS_PATH, = 300.
- Originating autonomous system = 300.
- Routes matched: 192.168.2.0.

```
Router#show ip bgp regexp ^200
```

- Match beginning of input string, AS_PATH, = 200.
- Last prepended autonomous system was 200.
- Routes matched: none.

Regular Expressions: Example Two

Use the following output of the **show ip bgp** command to see how different examples of regular expressions can help filter specific patterns.

```
Router#show ip bgp
   Network            Path
*> 192.168.0.0              i
*> 192.168.1.0       100 i
*> 192.168.3.0       100 200
i*> 192.168.4.0       300 i
*> 172.16.0.0        300 400 i
*> 10.0.0.0          300 400 1000 i
Router#show ip bgp regexp 100
```

- Match input string, AS_PATH, containing 100, including 1000.
- Routes matched: 192.168.1.0, 192.168.3.0, 10.0.0.0.

```
Router#show ip bgp regexp ^100_
```

- Match beginning of input string, AS_PATH, = 100.
- Last prepended autonomous system was 100.
- Routes matched: 192.168.1.0, 192.168.3.0.

BGP Route Filtering Using Access Lists

Figure 6-9 shows the commands necessary to configure route filters using access lists.

Figure 6-9   Network Topology for Route Filter Configuration Using Access Lists

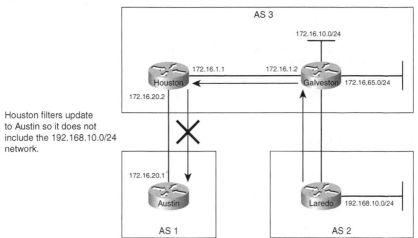

In this scenario, we want to have Houston filter updates to Austin so that it does not include the 192.69.10.0/24 network.

Houston(config)#**router bgp 3**	Starts the BGP routing process.
Houston(config-router)#**neighbor 172.16.1.2 remote-as 3**	Identifies a peer router at 172.16.1.2.
Houston(config-router)#**neighbor 172.16.20.1 remote-as 1**	Identifies a peer router at 172.16.20.1.
Houston(config-router)#**neighbor 172.16.20.1 distribute-list 1 out**	Applies a filter of ACL 1 to updates sent to neighbor 172.16.20.1.
Houston(config-router)#**exit**	Returns to global configuration mode.
Houston(config)#**access-list 1 deny 192.168.10.0 0.0.0.255**	Creates the filter to prevent the 192.168.10.0 network from being part of the routing update.
Houston(config)#**access-list 1 permit any**	Creates the filter that allows all other networks to be part of the routing update.

TIP: A standard ACL offers limited functionality. If you want to advertise the aggregate address of 172.16.0.0/16 but not the individual subnet, a standard ACL will not work. You need to use an extended ACL.

When you are using extended ACLS with BGP route filters, the extended ACL will first match the network address and *then* match the subnet mask of the prefix. To do this, both the network and the netmask are paired with their own wildcard bit-mask:

```
Router(config)#access-list 101 permit ip 172.16.0.0 0.0.255.255
255.255.0.0 0.0.0.0
```

To help overcome the confusing nature of this syntax, Cisco IOS Software intro-duced the **ip prefix-list** command in Cisco IOS Release 12.0.

BGP Route Filtering Using Prefix Lists

The general syntax for configuring a prefix list is as follows:

```
Router(config)#ip prefix-list list-name [seq seq-value] deny |
    permit network/len [ge ge-value] [le le-value]
```

The following table describes the parameters for this command.

Parameter	Description
list-name	The name of the prefix list.
seq	(Optional) Applies a sequence number to the entry being created or deleted.
seq-value	(Optional) Specifies the sequence number.
deny	Denies access to matching conditions.
permit	Permits access for matching conditions.
network/len	(Mandatory) The network number and length (in bits) of the netmask.
ge	(Optional) Applies *ge-value* to the range specified.
ge-value	(Optional) Specifies the lesser value of a range (the "from" portion of the range description).
le	(Optional) Applies *le-value* to the range specified.
le-value	(Optional) Specifies the greater value of a range (the "to" portion of the range description).

TIP: You must define a prefix list before you can apply it as a route filter.

TIP: There is an **implicit deny** statement at the end of each prefix list.

TIP: The range of sequence numbers that can be entered is from 1 to 4,294,967,294. If a sequence number is not entered when configuring this command, a default sequence numbering is applied to the prefix list. The number 5 is applied to the first prefix entry, and subsequent unnumbered entries are incremented by 5.

A router tests for prefix list matches from the lowest sequence number to the highest.

By numbering your **prefix-list** statements, you can add new entries at any point in the list.

The following examples show how you can use the **prefix-list** command to filter networks from being propagated through BGP.

`Router(config)#ip prefix-list KA-TET permit 172.16.0.0/16`	Creates an IP prefix list for BGP route filtering.
`Router(config)#router bgp 100`	Starts the BGP routing process.
`Router(config-router)#neighbor 192.168.1.1 remote-as 200`	Identifies a peer router at 192.168.1.1.
`Router(config-router)#neighbor 192.168.1.1 prefix-list KA-TET out`	Applies the prefix list named KA-TET to updates sent to this peer.
	NOTE: This configuration restricts the update to the 172.16.0.0/16 summary. The router will not send a subnet route—such as 172.16.0.0/17 or 172.16.20/24 in an update to autonomous system 200.
`Router(config)#ip prefix-list ROSE permit 192.0.0.0/8 le 24`	Creates a prefix list that will accept a netmask of up to 24 bits (**le** meaning less than or equal to) in routes with the prefix 192.0.0.0/8. Because no sequence number is identified, the default number of 5 is applied.
`Router(config)#ip prefix-list ROSE deny 192.0.0.0/8 ge 25`	Creates a prefix list that will deny routes with a netmask of 25 bits or greater (**ge** meaning greater than or equal to) in routes with the prefix 192.0.0.0/8. Because no sequence number is identified, the number 10 is applied—an increment of 5 over the previous statement.

	NOTE: This configuration will allow routes such as 192.2.0.0/16 or 192.2.20.0/24 to be permitted, but a more specific subnet such as 192.168.10.128/25 will be denied.
Router(config)#**ip prefix-list** TOWER **permit 10.0.0.0/8 ge 16 le 24**	Creates a prefix list that permits all prefixes in the 10.0.0.0/8 address space that have a netmask of between 16 and 24 bits (greater than or equal to 16 bits, and less than or equal to 24 bits).
Router(config)#**ip prefix-list** SHARDIK **seq 5 deny 0.0.0.0/0**	Creates a prefix list and assigns a sequence number of 5 to this statement.
Router(config)#**ip prefix-list** SHARDIK **seq 10 permit 172.16.0.0/16**	Creates a prefix list and assigns a sequence number of 10 to this statement.
Router(config)#**ip prefix-list** SHARDIK **seq 15 permit 192.168.0.0/16 le 24**	Creates a prefix list and assigns a sequence number of 15 to this statement.
Router(config)#**no ip prefix-list** SHARDIK **seq 10**	Removes sequence number 10 from the prefix list.

Configuration Example: BGP

Figure 6-10 shows the network topology for the configuration that follows, which demonstrates a simple BGP network using the commands covered in this chapter.

Figure 6-10   Network Topology for Simple BGP Network

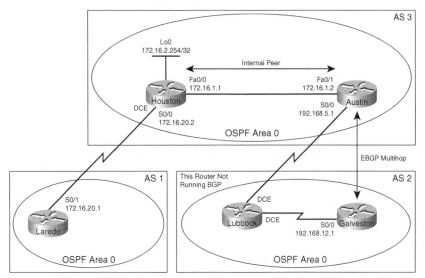

Houston Router

`Router>`**`enable`**	Moves to privileged mode.
`Router#`**`configure terminal`**	Moves to global configuration mode.
`Router(config)#`**`hostname Houston`**	Sets the router name to Houston.
`Houston(config)#`**`interface loopback 0`**	Moves to loopback interface mode.
`Houston(config-if)#`**`ip address`** **`172.16.2.254 255.255.255.255`**	Assigns an IP address and netmask.
`Houston(config-if)#`**`interface`** **`fastethernet 0/0`**	Moves to interface configuration mode.
`Houston(config-if)#`**`ip address`** **`172.16.1.1 255.255.255.0`**	Assigns an IP address and netmask.
`Houston(config-if)#`**`no shutdown`**	Enables the interface.
`Houston(config-if)#`**`interface serial`** **`0/0/0`**	Moves to interface configuration mode.
`Houston(config-if)#`**`ip address`** **`172.16.20.2 255.255.255.0`**	Assigns an IP address and netmask.
`Houston(config-if)#`**`clock rate 56000`**	Assigns the clock rate.

`Houston(config-if)#no shutdown`	Activates the interface.
`Houston(config-if)#exit`	Returns to global configuration mode.
`Houston(config)#router ospf 1`	Starts the OSPF routing process.
`Houston(config-router)#network 172.16.0.0 0.0.255.255 area 0`	Assigns any interface with an address of 172.16.*x.x* to be placed into OSPF area 0.
`Houston(config-router)#exit`	Returns to global configuration mode.
`Houston(config)#router bgp 3`	Starts the BGP routing process.
`Houston(config-router)#no synchronization`	Turns off route synchronization.
`Houston(config-router)#neighbor 172.16.1.2 remote-as 3`	Identifies a peer router at 172.16.1.2.
`Houston(config-router)#neighbor 172.16.1.2 update-source loopback 0`	Informs the router to use any operational interface for TCP connections, as long as Loopback0 is configured.
`Houston(config-router)#neighbor 172.16.20.1 remote-as 1`	Identifies a peer router at 172.16.20.1.
`Houston(config-router)#no auto-summary`	Disables auto-summarization.
`Houston(config-router)#exit`	Returns to global configuration mode.
`Houston(config)#exit`	Returns to privileged mode.
`Houston#copy running-config startup-config`	Saves the configuration to NVRAM.

Laredo Router

`Router>enable`	Moves to privileged mode.
`Router#configure terminal`	Moves to global configuration mode.
`Router(config)#hostname Laredo`	Sets the router name to Laredo.
`Laredo(config)#interface serial 0/0/1`	Moves to interface configuration mode.

Laredo(config-if)#ip address 172.16.20.1 255.255.255.0	Assigns an IP address and netmask.
Laredo(config-if)#no shutdown	Activates the interface.
Laredo(config-if)#exit	Returns to global configuration mode.
Laredo(config)#router bgp 1	Starts the BGP routing process.
Laredo(config-router)#no synchronization	Turns off route synchronization.
Laredo(config-router)#neighbor 172.16.20.2 remote-as 3	Identifies a peer router at 172.16.20.2.
Laredo(config-router)#no auto-summary	Disables auto-summarization.
Laredo(config-router)#exit	Returns to global configuration mode.
Laredo(config)#exit	Returns to privileged mode.
Laredo#copy running-config startup-config	Saves the configuration to NVRAM.

Galveston Router

Router>enable	Moves to privileged mode.
Router#configure terminal	Moves to global configuration mode.
Router(config)#hostname Galveston	Sets router name to Galveston.
Galveston(config)#interface serial 0/0/0	Moves to interface configuration mode.
Galveston(config-if)#ip address 192.168.12.1 255.255.255.0	Assigns an IP address and netmask.
Galveston(config-if)#no shutdown	Activates the interface.
Galveston(config-if)#exit	Returns to global configuration mode.
Galveston(config)#router ospf 1	Starts the OSPF routing process.

Galveston(config-router)#**network 192.168.12.0 0.0.0.255 area 0**	Assigns any interface with an address of 192.168.12.x to be placed into OSPF Area 0.
Galveston(config-router)#**exit**	Returns to global configuration mode.
Galveston(config)#**router bgp 2**	Starts the BGP routing process.
Galveston(config-router)#**neighbor 192.168.5.1 remote-as 3**	Identifies a peer router at 192.168.5.1.
Galveston(config-router)#**neighbor 192.168.5.1 ebgp-multihop 2**	Allows for two routers that are not directly connected to establish an EBGP session.
Galveston(config-router)#**no auto-summary**	Disables auto-summarization.
Galveston(config-router)#**exit**	Returns to global configuration mode.
Galveston(config)#**exit**	Returns to privileged mode.
Galveston#**copy running-config startup-config**	Saves the configuration to NVRAM.

Austin Router

Router>**enable**	Moves to privileged mode.
Router#**configure terminal**	Moves to global configuration mode.
Router(config)#**hostname Austin**	Sets the router name to Austin.
Austin(config)#**interface serial 0/0/0**	Moves to interface configuration mode.
Austin(config-if)#**ip address 192.168.5.1 255.255.255.0**	Assigns an IP address and netmask.
Austin(config-if)#**no shutdown**	Activates the interface.
Austin(config-if)#**interface fastethernet 0/1**	Moves to interface configuration mode.

Austin (config-if)#**ip address 172.16.1.2 255.255.255.0**	Assigns an IP address and netmask.
Austin(config-if)#**no shutdown**	Activates the interface.
Austin(config-if)#**exit**	Returns to global configuration mode.
Austin(config)#**router ospf 1**	Starts the OSPF routing process.
Austin(config-router)#**network 172.16.0.0 0.0.255.255 area 0**	Assigns any interface with an address of 172.16.*x*.*x* to be placed into OSPF area 0.
Austin(config-router)#**network 192.168.5.0 0.0.0.255 area 0**	Assigns any interface with an address of 192.168.5.*x* to be placed into OSPF area 0.
Austin(config-router)#**exit**	Returns to global configuration mode.
Austin(config)#**router bgp 3**	Starts the BGP routing process.
Austin(config-router)#**no synchronization**	Turns off route synchronization.
Austin(config-router)#**neighbor 172.16.2.254 remote-as 3**	Identifies a peer router at 172.16.2.254.
Austin(config-router)#**neighbor 192.168.12.1 remote-as 2**	Identifies a peer router at 192.168.12.1.
Austin(config-router)#**neighbor 192.168.12.1 ebgp-multihop 2**	Allows for two routers that are not directly connected to establish an eBGP session.
Austin(config-router)#**no auto-summary**	Turns off auto-summarization.
Austin(config-router)#**exit**	Returns to global configuration mode.
Austin(config)#**exit**	Returns to privileged mode.
Austin#**copy running-config startup-config**	Saves the configuration to NVRAM.

CHAPTER 7

Implementing IPv6

This chapter provides information and commands concerning the following implementing IPv6 topics:

- Assigning IPv6 addresses to interfaces
- IPv6 on NBMA networks
- Cisco Express Forwarding (CEF) and distributed CEF (dCEF) switching for IPv6
- IPv6 and RIPng
- Configuration example: IPv6 RIP
- IPv6 and OSPFv3
  - Enabling OSPF for IPv6 on an interface
  - OSPFv3 and stub/NSSA areas
  - Enabling an OSPF for IPv6 area range
  - Enabling an IPv4 router ID for OSPFv3
  - Forcing an SPF calculation
- Configuration example: OSPFv3
- IPv6 and EIGRP
  - Enabling EIGRP for IPv6 on an interface
  - Configuring the percentage of link bandwidth used by EIGRP
  - Configuring summary addresses
  - Configuring EIGRP route authentication
  - Configuring EIGRP timers
  - Configuring EIGRP stub routing
  - Logging EIGRP neighbor adjacency changes
  - Adjusting the EIGRP for IPv6 metric weights
- Route redistribution
- IPv6 transition techniques
  - Configuring manual IPv6 tunnels
  - Configuring Generic Routing Encapsulation IPv6 tunnels
  - Configuring automatic 6to4 tunnels
  - Configuring IPv4-compatible IPv6 tunnels
  - Configuring ISATAP tunnels
  - Verifying IPv6 tunnel configuration and operation
- Implementing NAT-PT for IPv6
  - Configuring basic IPv6 to IPv4 connectivity for NAT-PT for IPv6
  - Configuring IPv4-mapped NAT-PT

— Configuring mappings for IPv6 hosts accessing IPv4 hosts

— Configuring IPv6 access control lists

— Configuring mappings for IPv4 hosts accessing IPv6 hosts

— Configuring Port Address Translation for IPv6 to IPv4 address mappings

— Verifying NAT-PT configuration and operation

- Static routes in IPv6

- Floating static routes in IPv6

- Verifying and troubleshooting IPv6

- IPv6 PING

NOTE: For an excellent overview of IPv6, we strongly recommend you read Jeff Doyle's book, *Routing TCP/IP,* Volume I, Second Edition.

Assigning IPv6 Addresses to Interfaces

Router(config)#**ipv6 unicast-routing**	Enables the forwarding of IPv6 unicast datagrams globally on the router.
Router(config)#**interface fastethernet 0/0**	Moves to interface configuration mode.
Router(config-if)#**ipv6 enable**	Automatically configures an IPv6 link-local address on the interface and enables IPv6 processing on the interface.
	NOTE: The link-local address that the **ipv6 enable** command configures can be used only to communicate with nodes on the same link.
Router(config-if)#**ipv6 address autoconfig**	Router will configure itself with a link-local address using stateless auto-configuration.
Router(config-if)#**ipv6 address 3000::1/64**	Configures a global IPv6 address on the interface and enables IPv6 processing on the interface.

Router(config-if)#**ipv6 address 2001:db8:0:1::/64 eui-64**	Configures a global IPv6 address with an interface identifier in the low-order 64 bits of the IPv6 address.
Router(config-if)#**ipv6 address fe80::260:3eff:fe47:1530/64 link-local**	Configures a specific link-local IPv6 address on the interface rather than the one that is automatically configured when IPv6 is enabled on the interface.
Router(config-if)#**ipv6 unnumbered** *type/ number*	Specifies an unnumbered interface and enables IPv6 processing on the interface. The global IPv6 address of the interface specified by *type/ number* will be used as the source address.
Router(config-if)#**ipv6 nd reachable-time** *x*	Configures the amount of time that a remote IPv6 node is considered reachable after some reachability confirmation event has occurred. Measured in milliseconds.

NOTE: 0 milliseconds (unspecified) is advertised in router advertisements and the value 30 000 (30 seconds) is used for the neighbor discovery activity of the router itself. IPv6 addresses can be configured on a router without first configuring ipv6 unicast routing. However, if this occurs, the router will act more like an IPv6 host and will not forward IPv6 packets.

IPv6 on NBMA Networks

The behavior of IPv6 unicast forwarding on Frame Relay networks is the same as IPv4 unicast forwarding. There are, however, two big differences when configuring IPv6 for unicast forwarding:

- You must configure mappings for link-local addresses because they will often be used by control plane operations such as routing protocols. The link-local address is used as the next-hop address for any routes installed in the routing table by an Interior Gateway Protocol. If the next-hop link-local address is not reachable because it is not mapped to the correct data-link connection identifier (DLCI), the remote network will be unreachable. Use the **frame-relay map ipv6** command in interface configuration mode to achieve this.

- You must explicitly enable IPv6 unicast routing using the **ipv6 unicast-routing** global configuration command when you attempt to ping from one spoke to another spoke on a hub-and-spoke topology.

Cisco Express Forwarding (CEF) and Distributed CEF (dCEF) Switching for IPv6

`Router(config)#ipv6 cef`	Enables CEFv6 globally on the router.
	NOTE: You must enable CEFv4 globally on the router by using the **ip cef** global configuration command before enabling CEFv6 globally on the router.
	NOTE: The **ipv6 cef** command is not supported on the Cisco 12000 series Internet routers because this distributed platform operates only in dCEFv6 mode.
`Router(config)#ipv6 cef distributed`	Enables dCEFv6 globally on the router.
	NOTE: You must enable dCEFv4 by using the **ip cef distributed** global configuration command before enabling dCEFv6 globally on the router.
	NOTE: The **ipv6 cef distributed** command is not supported on the Cisco 12000 series Internet routers because dCEFv6 is enabled by default on this platform.
`Router(config)#ipv6 cef accounting per-prefix`	Enables CEFv6 and dCEFv6 network accounting globally on the router. The keyword **per-prefix** enables the collection of the number of packets and bytes express forwarded to an IPv6 destination or IPv6 prefix.

`Router(config)#`**`ipv6 cef accounting prefix-length`**	Enables CEFv6 and dCEFv6 network accounting globally on the router. The keyword **prefix-length** enables the collection of the number of packets and bytes forwarded to an IPv6 prefix length.
	NOTE: When CEFv6 is enabled globally on the router, accounting information is collected at the route processor (RP); when dCEFv6 is enabled globally on the router, accounting information is collected at the line cards.

IPv6 and RIPng

`Router(config)#`**`ipv6 unicast-routing`**	Enables the forwarding of IPv6 unicast datagrams globally on the router.
`Router(config)#`**`interface serial 0/0/0`**	Moves to interface configuration mode.
`Router(config-if)#`**`ipv6 rip tower enable`**	Creates the RIPng process named tower and enables RIPng on the interface.
	NOTE: Unlike RIPv1 and RIPv2, where you needed to create the RIP routing process with the **router rip** command and then use the **network** command to specify the interfaces on which to run RIP, the RIPng process is created automatically when RIPng is enabled on an interface with the **ipv6 rip** *name* **enable** command.
	NOTE: Cisco IOS software automatically creates an entry in the configuration for the RIPng routing process when it is enabled on an interface.
	NOTE: The **ipv6 router rip** *process-name* command is still needed when configuring optional features of RIPng.

`Router(config)#ipv6 router rip tower`	Creates the RIPng process named tower if it has not already been created, and moves to router configuration mode.
`Router(config-router)#maximum-paths 2`	Defines the maximum number of equal-cost routes that RIPng can support.
	NOTE: The number of paths that can be used is a number from 1 to 64. The default is 4.

Configuration Example: IPv6 RIP

Figure 7-1 illustrates the network topology for the configuration that follows, which shows how to configure IPv6 and RIPng using the commands covered in this chapter.

Figure 7-1   Network Topology for IPv6/RIPng Configuration Example

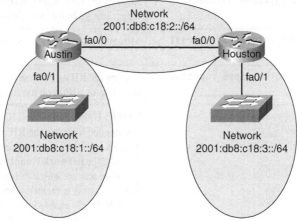

Austin Router

`Router>enable`	Moves to privileged mode.
`Router#configure terminal`	Moves to global configuration mode.
`Router(config)#hostname Austin`	Assigns a hostname to the router.
`Austin(config)#ipv6 unicast-routing`	Enables the forwarding of IPv6 unicast datagrams globally on the router.

`Austin(config)#interface fastethernet 0/0`	Enters interface configuration mode.
`Austin(config-if)#ipv6 enable`	Automatically configures an IPv6 link-local address on the interface and enables IPv6 processing on the interface.
`Austin(config-if)#ipv6 address 2001:db8:c18:2::/64 eui-64`	Configures a global IPv6 address with an interface identifier in the low-order 64 bits of the IPv6 address.
`Austin(config-if)#ipv6 rip tower enable`	Creates the RIPng process named tower and enables RIPng on the interface.
`Austin(config-if)#no shutdown`	Enables the interface.
`Austin(config-if)#interface fastethernet 0/1`	Enters interface configuration mode.
`Austin(config-if)#ipv6 enable`	Automatically configures an IPv6 link-local address on the interface and enables IPv6 processing on the interface.
`Austin(config-if)#ipv6 address 2001:db8:c18:1::/64 eui-64`	Configures a global IPv6 address with an interface identifier in the low-order 64 bits of the IPv6 address.
`Austin(config-if)#ipv6 rip tower enable`	Creates the RIPng process named tower and enables RIPng on the interface.
`Austin(config-if)#no shutdown`	Enables the interface.
`Austin(config-if)#exit`	Moves to global configuration mode.
`Austin(config)#exit`	Moves to privileged mode.
`Austin#copy running-config startup-config`	Saves the configuration to NVRAM.

Houston Router

`Router>enable`	Moves to privileged mode.
`Router#configure terminal`	Moves to global configuration mode.
`Router(config)#hostname Houston`	Assigns a hostname to the router.
`Houston(config)#ipv6 unicast-routing`	Enables the forwarding of IPv6 unicast datagrams globally on the router.

`Houston(config)#interface fastethernet 0/0`	Enters interface configuration mode.
`Houston(config-if)#ipv6 enable`	Automatically configures an IPv6 link-local address on the interface and enables IPv6 processing on the interface.
`Houston(config-if)#ipv6 address 2001:db8:c18:2::/64 eui-64`	Configures a global IPv6 address with an interface identifier in the low-order 64 bits of the IPv6 address.
`Houston(config-if)#ipv6 rip tower enable`	Creates the RIPng process named tower and enables RIPng on the interface.
`Houston(config-if)#no shutdown`	Enables the interface.
`Houston(config-if)#interface fastethernet 0/1`	Enters interface configuration mode.
`Houston(config-if)#ipv6 enable`	Automatically configures an IPv6 link-local address on the interface and enables IPv6 processing on the interface.
`Houston(config-if)#ipv6 address 2001:db8:c18:3::/64 eui-64`	Configures a global IPv6 address with an interface identifier in the low-order 64 bits of the IPv6 address.
`Houston(config-if)#ipv6 rip tower enable`	Creates the RIPng process named tower and enables RIPng on the interface
`Houston(config-if)#no shutdown`	Enables the interface.
`Houston(config-if)#exit`	Moves to global configuration mode.
`Houston(config)#exit`	Moves to privileged mode.
`Houston#copy running-config startup-config`	Saves the configuration to NVRAM.

IPv6 and OSPFv3

Working with IPv6 requires modifications to any dynamic protocol. The current version of Open Shortest Path First (OSPF), OSPFv2, was developed back in the late 1980s, when some parts of OSPF were designed to compensate for the inefficiencies of routers at that time. Now that router technology has dramatically increased, rather than modify OSPFv2 for IPv6, it was decided to create a new version of OSPF—OSPFv3—not just for IPv6, but for other, newer technologies, too. This section covers using IPv6 with OSPFv3.

Enabling OSPF for IPv6 on an Interface

`Router(config)#ipv6 unicast-routing`	Enables the forwarding of IPv6 unicast datagrams globally on the router.
`Router(config)#interface fastethernet 0/0`	Moves to interface configuration mode.
`Router(config-if)#ipv6 address 2001:db8:0:1::/64`	Configures a global IPv6 address on the interface and enables IPv6 processing on the interface.
`Router(config-if)#ipv6 ospf 1 area 0`	Enables OSPFv3 process 1 on the interface and places this interface into area 0.
	NOTE: The OSPFv3 process is created automatically when OSPFv3 is enabled on an interface.
	NOTE: The **ipv6 ospf** *x* **area** *y* command has to be configured on each interface that will take part in OSPFv3.
`Router(config-if)#ipv6 ospf priority 30`	Assigns a priority number to this interface for use in the designated router (DR) election. The priority can be a number from 0 to 255. The default is 1. A router with a priority set to 0 is ineligible to become the DR or the backup DR (BDR).
`Router(config-if)#ipv6 ospf cost 20`	Assigns a cost value of 20 to this interface. The cost value can be an integer value from 1 to 65,535.

OSPFv3 and Stub/NSSA Areas

`Router(config)#ipv6 router ospf`	Creates the OSPFv3 process if it has not already been created, and moves to router configuration mode.
`Router(config-router)#area 1 stub`	The router is configured to be part of a stub area.

Router(config-router)#area 1 stub no-summary	The router is configured to be in a totally stubby area. This router is the Area Border Router (ABR) due to the **no-summary** keyword.
Router(config-router)#area 1 nssa	The router is configured to be in a not-so-stubby area (NSSA).
Router(config-router)#area 1 nssa no-summary	The router is configured to be in a totally stubby, NSSA area. This router is the ABR due to the **no-summary** keyword.

Enabling an OSPF for IPv6 Area Range

Router(config)#ipv6 router ospf	Creates the OSPFv3 process if it has not already been created, and moves to router configuration mode.
Router(config-router)#area 1 range 2001:db8::/48	Consolidates and summarizes routes at an area boundary.

Enabling an IPv4 Router ID for OSPFv3

Router(config)#ipv6 router ospf	Creates the OSPFv3 process if it has not already been created, and moves to router configuration mode.
Router(config-router)#router-id 192.168.254.255	Creates an IPv4 32-bit router ID for this router.
	NOTE: In OSPF for IPv6, it is possible that no IPv4 addresses will be configured on any interface. In this case, the user must use the **router-id** command to configure a router ID before the OSPF process will be started. If an IPv4 address does exist when OSPF for IPv6 is enabled on an interface, that IPv4 address is used for the router ID. If more than one IPv4 address is available, a router ID is chosen using the same rules as for OSPF Version 2.

Forcing an SPF Calculation

`Router#clear ipv6 ospf 1 process`	The OSPF database is cleared and repopulated, and then the SPF algorithm is performed.
`Router#clear ipv6 ospf 1 force-spf`	The OSPF database is not cleared; just an SPF calculation is performed.

CAUTION: As with OSPFv2, clearing the OSPFv3 database and forcing a recalculation of the Shortest Path First (SPF) algorithm is processor intensive and should be used with caution.

Configuration Example: OSPFv3

Figure 7-2 shows the network topology for the configuration that follows, which demonstrates how to configure IPv6 and OSPFv3 using the commands covered in this chapter.

Figure 7-2   Network Topology for IPv6 and OSPFv3 Configuration

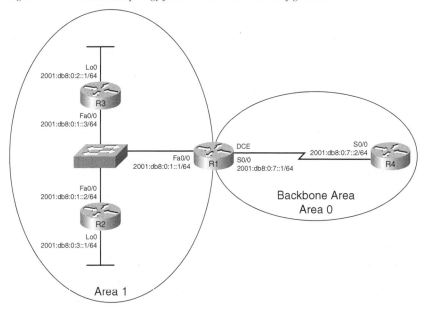

R3 Router

Router>`enable`	Moves to privileged mode.
Router#`configure terminal`	Moves to global configuration mode.
Router(config)#`hostname R3`	Assigns a hostname to the router.
R3(config)#`ipv6 unicast-routing`	Enables the forwarding of IPv6 unicast datagrams globally on the router.
R3(config)#`interface fastethernet 0/0`	Moves to interface configuration mode.
R3(config-if)#`ipv6 address` `2001:db8:0:1::3/64`	Configures a global IPv6 address on the interface and enables IPv6 processing on the interface.
R3(config-if)#`ipv6 ospf 1 area 1`	Enables OSPFv3 on the interface and places this interface into area 1.
R3(config-if)#`no shutdown`	Enables the interface.
R3(config-if)#`interface loopback 0`	Moves to interface configuration mode.
R3(config-if)#`ipv6 address` `2001:db8:0:2::1/64`	Configures a global IPv6 address on the interface and enables IPv6 processing on the interface.
R3(config-if)#`ipv6 ospf 1 area 1`	Enables OSPFv3 on the interface and places this interface into area 1.
R3(config-if)#`exit`	Moves to global configuration mode.
R3(config)#`exit`	Moves to privileged mode.
R3#`copy running-config startup-config`	Saves the configuration to NVRAM.

R2 Router

Router>`enable`	Moves to privileged mode.
Router#`configure terminal`	Moves to global configuration mode.

Router(config)#**hostname R2**	Assigns a hostname to the router.
R2(config)#**ipv6 unicast-routing**	Enables the forwarding of IPv6 unicast datagrams globally on the router.
R2(config)#**interface fastethernet 0/0**	Moves to interface configuration mode.
R2(config-if)#**ipv6 address 2001:db8:0:1::2/64**	Configures a global IPv6 address on the interface and enables IPv6 processing on the interface.
R2(config-if)#**ipv6 ospf 1 area 1**	Enables OSPFv3 on the interface and places this interface into area 1.
R2(config-if)#**no shutdown**	Enables the interface.
R2(config-if)#**interface loopback 0**	Moves to interface configuration mode.
R2(config-if)#**ipv6 address 2001:db8:0:3::1/64**	Configures a global IPv6 address on the interface and enables IPv6 processing on the interface.
R2(config-if)#**ipv6 ospf 1 area 1**	Enables OSPFv3 on the interface and places this interface into area 1.
R2(config-if)#**no shutdown**	Enables the interface.
R2(config-if)#**exit**	Moves to global configuration mode.
R2(config)#**exit**	Moves to privileged mode.
R2#**copy running-config startup-config**	Saves the configuration to NVRAM.

R1 Router

Router>**enable**	Moves to privileged mode.
Router#**configure terminal**	Moves to global configuration mode.
Router(config)#**hostname R1**	Assigns a hostname to the router.

`R1(config)#ipv6 unicast-routing`	Enables the forwarding of IPv6 unicast datagrams globally on the router.
`R1(config)#interface fastethernet 0/0`	Moves to interface configuration mode.
`R1(config-if)#ipv6 address 2001:db8:0:1::1/64`	Configures a global IPv6 address on the interface and enables IPv6 processing on the interface.
`R1(config-if)#ipv6 ospf 1 area 1`	Enables OSPFv3 on the interface and places this interface into area 1.
`R1(config-if)#no shutdown`	Enables the interface.
`R1(config-if)#interface serial 0/0/0`	Moves to interface configuration mode.
`R1(config-if)#ipv6 address 2001:db8:0:7::1/64`	Configures a global IPv6 address on the interface and enables IPv6 processing on the interface.
`R1(config-if)#ipv6 ospf 1 area 0`	Enables OSPFv3 on the interface and places this interface into area 0.
`R1(config-if)#clock rate 56000`	Assigns a clock rate to this interface.
`R1(config-if)#no shutdown`	Enables the interface.
`R1(config-if)#exit`	Moves to global configuration mode.
`R1(config)#exit`	Moves to privileged mode.
`R1#copy running-config startup-config`	Saves the configuration to NVRAM.

R4 Router

`Router>enable`	Moves to privileged mode.
`Router#configure terminal`	Moves to global configuration mode.
`Router(config)#hostname R4`	Assigns a hostname to the router.
`R4(config)#ipv6 unicast-routing`	Enables the forwarding of IPv6 unicast datagrams globally on the router.

R4(config)#interface serial 0/0/0	Moves to interface configuration mode.
R4(config-if)#ipv6 address 2001:db8:0:7::2/64	Configures a global IPv6 address on the interface and enables IPv6 processing on the interface.
R4(config-if)#ipv6 ospf 1 area 0	Enables OSPFv3 on the interface and places this interface into area 1.
R4(config-if)#no shutdown	Enables the interface.
R4(config-if)#exit	Moves to global configuration mode.
R4(config)#exit	Moves to privileged mode.
R4#copy running-config startup-config	Saves the configuration to NVRAM.

IPv6 and EIGRP

You can now configure EIGRP to route IPv6 prefixes. There is no linkage between EIGRP for IPv4 and EIGRP for IPv6; they are configured and managed separately. However, the commands for configuration of EIGRP for IPv4 and IPv6 are very similar, making the transition very easy.

Enabling EIGRP for IPv6 on an Interface

Router(config)#ipv6 unicast-routing	Enables the forwarding of IPv6 unicast datagrams globally on the router.
Router(config)#interface serial 0/0/0	Moves to interface configuration mode.
Router(config-if)#ipv6 eigrp 100	Enables IPv6 processing on an interface that has not been configured with an explicit IPv6 address.
Router(config-if)#ipv6 router eigrp 100	Enters router configuration mode and creates an EIGRP IPv6 routing process.
Router(config-router)#eigrp router-id 10.1.1.1	Enables the use of a fixed router ID.

NOTE: Use the **eigrp router-id w.x.y.z** command only if an IPv4 address is not defined on the router eligible for router ID.

NOTE: EIGRP for IPv6 can also be created by entering into router configuration mode and creating the router process, just like you would with EIGRP for IPv4. However, the EIGRP for IPv6 process starts in shutdown mode. Therefore, you need to add the **no shutdown** command to your configuration in order for EIGRP for IPv6 to start:

```
Router(config)#ipv6 router eigrp 400
Router(config-router)#eigrp router-id 10.1.1.1
Router(config-router)#no shutdown
```

Configuring the Percentage of Link Bandwidth Used by EIGRP

Router(config)#**interface serial 0/0/0**	Moves to interface configuration mode.
Router(config-if)#**ipv6 bandwidth-percent eigrp 100 75**	Configures the percentage of bandwidth (75%) that may be used by EIGRP for IPv6 on the interface.

Configuring Summary Addresses

Router(config)#**interface serial 0/0/0**	Moves to interface configuration mode.
Router(config-if)#**ipv6 summary-address eigrp 100 2001:0DB8:0:1::/64**	Configures a summary aggregate address for a specified interface.

Configuring EIGRP Route Authentication

Router(config)#**interface serial 0/0/0**	Moves to interface configuration mode.
Router(config-if)#**ipv6 authentication mode eigrp 100 md5**	Specifies the type of authentication used in EIGRP for IPv6 packets. In this case, we are using MD5.
Router(config-if)#**ipv6 authentication key-chain eigrp 100 chain1**	Enables authentication of EIGRP over IPv6 packets.

Router(config-if)#**exit**	Returns to global configuration mode.
Router(config)#**key chain chain1**	Identifies a group of authentication keys. **chain1** matches the name of the key chain identified in interface configuration mode.
Router(config-keychain)#**key 1**	Identifies an authentication key on a key chain.
Router(config-keychain-key)#**key-string chain1**	Specifies the authentication string for a key.
Router(config-keychain-key)#**accept-lifetime 14:30:00 Jan 20 2010 duration 7200**	Sets the time period during which the authentication key on the key chain is received as valid.
Router(config-keychain-key)#**send-lifetime 15:00:00 Jan 20 2010 duration 36000**	Sets the time period during which an authentication key on a key chain is valid to be sent.

Configuring EIGRP Timers

Router(config)#**interface serial 0/0/0**	Moves to interface configuration mode.
Router(config-if)#**ipv6 hello-interval eigrp 100 10**	Configures the hello interval for EIGRP for IPv6 process 100 to be 10 seconds.
Router(config-if)#**ipv6 hold-time eigrp 100 40**	Configures the hold timer for EIGRP for IPv6 process 100 to be 40 seconds.

Configuring EIGRP Stub Routing

Router(config)#**ipv6 router eigrp 100**	Enters router configuration mode and creates an EIGRP IPv6 routing process.
Router(config-router)#**eigrp stub**	Configures a router as a stub using EIGRP.

Logging EIGRP Neighbor Adjacency Changes

Router(config)#ipv6 router eigrp 100	Enters router configuration mode and creates an EIGRP IPv6 routing process.
Router(config-router)#eigrp log-neighbor changes	Enables the logging of changes in EIGRP for IPv6 neighbor adjacencies.
Router(config-router)#eigrp log-neighbor-warnings 300	Configures the logging intervals of EIGRP neighbor warning messages to 300 seconds.

Adjusting the EIGRP for IPv6 Metric Weights

Router(config)#ipv6 router eigrp 100	Enters router configuration mode and creates an EIGRP IPv6 routing process.
Router(config-router)#metric weights *tos k1 k2 k3 k4 k5*	Changes the default *k* values used in metric calculation. These are the default values: tos=0, k1=1, k2=0, k3=1, k4=0, k5=0

Route Redistribution

Router(config)#ipv6 unicast-routing	Enables the forwarding of IPv6 unicast datagrams globally on the router.
Router(config)#interface serial 0/0/0	Moves to interface configuration mode.
Router(config-if)#ipv6 rip tower enable	Creates the RIPng process named tower and enables RIPng on the interface.
Router(config-if)#redistribute *protocol* [*process-id*] {level-1 I level-1-2 I level-2} [metric *metric-value*] [metric-type {internal I external}] [route-map *map-name*]	Redistributes the specified routes into the IPv6 RIP routing process.

NOTE: When using the redistribute command, the protocol argument can be one of the following keywords: bgp, connected, eigrp, isis, ospf, rip, or static.

NOTE: When using the redistribute command, the syntax differs slightly depending on the routing protocol into which routes will be redistributed.

IPv6 Transition Techniques

Because of the sheer number of IPv4-based networks in the world today, transitioning from IPv4 to IPv6 is going to take place over a very long period of time, with a great deal of coexistence between the two protocols. The following sections list five different methods of tunneling IPv6 packets inside of IPv4 packets as a transition technique.

Configuring Manual IPv6 Tunnels

In manually configured IPv6 tunnels, an IPv6 address is configured on a tunnel interface and manually configured IPv4 addresses are assigned to the tunnel source and tunnel destination. The host or router at each end of a configured tunnel must support both the IPv4 and IPv6 protocol stacks.

Figure 7-3 shows the network topology for the configuration that follows, which demonstrates how IPv6 tunnels are created.

Figure 7-3   Network Topology for IPv6 Tunnel Configuration

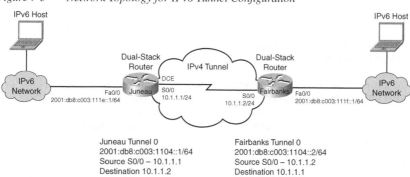

Juneau Router

`Router>`**`enable`**	Moves to privileged mode.
`Router#`**`configure terminal`**	Moves to global configuration mode.
`Router(config)#`**`hostname Juneau`**	Sets the hostname of the router.
`Juneau(config)#`**`ipv6 unicast-routing`**	Enables the forwarding of IPv6 unicast datagrams globally on the router.

`Juneau(config)#ip cef`	Enables CEFv4 globally on the router.
`Juneau(config)#ipv6 cef`	Enables CEFv6 globally on the router.
`Juneau(config)#interface tunnel0`	Moves to tunnel interface configuration mode.
`Juneau(config-if)#ipv6 address 2001:db8:c003:1104::1/64`	Assigns the IPv6 address to this interface.
`Juneau(config-if)#tunnel source serial 0/0/0`	Specifies the source interface type and number for the tunnel interface.
`Juneau(config-if)#tunnel destination 10.1.1.2`	Specifies the destination IPv4 address for the tunnel interface.
`Juneau(config-if)#tunnel mode ipv6ip`	Specifies a manual IPv6 tunnel—specifically that IPv6 is the passenger protocol and IPv4 is both the encapsulation and protocol for the IPv6 tunnel.
`Juneau(config-if)#interface fastethernet 0/0`	Moves to interface configuration mode.
`Juneau(config-if)#ipv6 address 2001:db8:c003:111e::1/64`	Assigns an IPv6 address to this interface.
`Juneau(config-if)#no shutdown`	Enables the interface.
`Juneau(config-if)#interface serial 0/0/0`	Moves to interface configuration mode.
`Juneau(config-if)#ip address 10.1.1.1 255.255.255.252`	Assigns an IPv4 address and netmask.
`Juneau(config-if)#clock rate 56000`	Sets the clock rate on the interface.
`Juneau(config-if)#no shutdown`	Enables the interface.
`Juneau(config-if)#exit`	Moves to global configuration mode.
`Juneau(config)#exit`	Moves to privileged mode.
`Juneau#copy running-config startup-config`	Saves the configuration to NVRAM.

Fairbanks Router

`Router>enable`	Moves to privileged mode.
`Router#configure terminal`	Moves to global configuration mode.
`Router(config)#hostname Fairbanks`	Sets the hostname of the router.
`Fairbanks(config)#ipv6 unicast-routing`	Enables the forwarding of IPv6 unicast datagrams globally on the router.
`Fairbanks(config)#ip cef`	Enables CEFv4 globally on the router.
`Fairbanks(config)#ipv6 cef`	Enables CEFv6 globally on the router.
`Fairbanks(config)#interface tunnel0`	Moves to tunnel interface configuration mode.
`Fairbanks(config-if)#ipv6 address 2001:db8:c003:1104::2/64`	Assigns an IPv6 address to this interface.
`Fairbanks(config-if)#tunnel source 10.1.1.2`	Specifies the IP address for the tunnel interface.
`Fairbanks(config-if)#tunnel destination 10.1.1.1`	Specifies the destination IPv4 address for the tunnel interface.
`Fairbanks(config-if)#tunnel mode ipv6ip`	Specifies a manual IPv6 tunnel—specifically that IPv6 is the passenger protocol and IPv4 is both the encapsulation and protocol for the IPv6 tunnel.
`Fairbanks(config-if)#interface fastethernet 0/0`	Moves to interface configuration mode.
`Fairbanks(config-if)#ipv6 address 2001:db8:c003:111f::1/64`	Assigns an IPv6 address to this interface.
`Fairbanks(config-if)#no shut`	Starts the interface.
`Fairbanks(config-if)#interface serial 0/0/0`	Moves to serial interface configuration mode.

Fairbanks(config-if)#ip address 10.1.1.2 255.255.255.252	Assigns an IPv4 address and netmask.
Fairbanks(config-if)#no shutdown	Enables the interface.
Fairbanks(config-if)#exit	Moves to global configuration mode.
Fairbanks(config)#exit	Moves to privileged mode.
Fairbanks#copy running-config startup-config	Saves the configuration to NVRAM.

Configuring Generic Routing Encapsulation IPv6 Tunnels

Generic Routing Encapsulation (GRE) tunnels can be configured to run over an IPv6 network layer and to transport IPv6 packets in IPv6 tunnels and IPv4 packets in IPv6 tunnels.

When GRE IPv6 tunnels are configured, IPv6 addresses are assigned to the tunnel source and the tunnel destination. The tunnel interface can have either IPv4 or IPv6 addresses assigned. The host or router at each end of a configured tunnel must support both the IPv4 and IPv6 protocol stacks.

Router#configure terminal	Enters global configuration mode.
Router(config)#ipv6 unicast-routing	Enables the forwarding of IPv6 unicast datagrams globally on the router.
Router(config)#ip cef	Enables CEFv4 globally on the router.
Router(config)#ipv6 cef	Enables CEFv6 globally on the router.
Router(config)#interface tunnel0	Moves to tunnel interface configuration mode.
Router(config-if)#ipv6 address 2001:db8:c003:111f::1/64	Assigns an IPv6 address to this interface.
Router(config-if)#tunnel source serial 0/0	Specifies the source interface type and number for the tunnel interface.
Router(config-if)#tunnel destination 10.1.1.1	Specifies the destination IPv4 address for the tunnel interface.
Router(config-if)#tunnel mode gre ipv6	Specifies a GRE IPv6 tunnel. This command specifies GRE as the encapsulation protocol for the tunnel.

Configuring Automatic 6to4 Tunnels

In 6to4 tunnels, the tunnel destination is determined by the border router IPv4 address, which is concatenated to the prefix 2002::/16 in the format **2002:***border-router-IPv4-address***::/48**. The border router at each end of a 6to4 tunnel must support both the IPv4 and IPv6 protocol stacks.

> **CAUTION:**   The configuration of only one IPv4-compatible tunnel and one 6to4 IPv6 tunnel is supported on a router. If you choose to configure both tunnel types on the same router, it is strongly recommended that they do not share the same tunnel source. This is because both tunnel types are NBMA point-to-multipoint access links and only the tunnel source can be used to reorder the packets from a multiplexed packet stream into a single packet stream for an incoming interface. When a packet with an IPv4 protocol type of 41 arrives on an interface, that packet is mapped to an IPv6 tunnel interface based on the IPv4 address. However, if both the 6to4 tunnel and the IPv4-compatible tunnel share the same source interface, the router is not able to determine the IPv6 tunnel interface to which it should assign the incoming packet. IPv6 manually configured tunnels can share the same source interface because a manual tunnel is a point-to-point link, and both the IPv4 source and IPv4 destination of the tunnel are defined.

Router#**configure terminal**	Enters global configuration mode.
Router(config)#**ipv6 unicast-routing**	Enables the forwarding of IPv6 unicast datagrams globally on the router.
Router(config)#**ip cef**	Enables CEFv4 globally on the router.
Router(config)#**ipv6 cef**	Enables CEFv6 globally on the router.
Router(config)#**interface tunnel0**	Moves to tunnel interface configuration mode.
Router(config-if)#**ipv6 address 2002:c0a8:6301:1::1/64**	Assigns an IPv6 address to this interface. The 32 bits following the 2002::/16 prefix (c0a8:6301) correspond to the IPv4 address assigned to the tunnel source (192.168.99.1).
Router(config-if)#**tunnel source serial 0/0**	Specifies the source interface type and number for the tunnel interface.
Router(config-if)#**tunnel mode ipv6ip 6to4**	Specifies an IPv6 overlay tunnel using a 6to4 address.
Router(config-if)#**exit**	Returns to global configuration mode.
Router(config)#**ipv6 route 2002::/16 tunnel0**	Configures a static route for the IPv6 6to4 prefix 2002::/16 to the specified tunnel interface.

NOTE: When configuring a 6to4 overlay tunnel, you must configure a static route for the IPv6 6to4 prefix 2002::/16 to the 6to4 tunnel interface.

NOTE: The tunnel number specified in the ipv6 route command must be the same tunnel number specified in the interface tunnel command.

Configuring IPv4-Compatible IPv6 Tunnels

With an IPv4-compatible tunnel, the tunnel destination is automatically determined by the IPv4 address in the low-order 32 bits of IPv4-compatible IPv6 addresses. The host or router at each end of a configured tunnel must support both the IPv4 and IPv6 protocol stacks.

`Router#configure terminal`	Enters global configuration mode.
`Router(config)#ipv6 unicast-routing`	Enables the forwarding of IPv6 unicast datagrams globally on the router.
`Router(config)#ip cef`	Enables CEFv4 globally on the router.
`Router(config)#ipv6 cef`	Enables CEFv6 globally on the router.
`Router(config)#interface tunnel0`	Moves to tunnel interface configuration mode.
`Router(config-if)#tunnel source serial 0/0/0`	Specifies the source interface type and number for the tunnel interface.
	NOTE: The interface type and number specified in the **tunnel source** command is configured with an IPv4 address only.
`Router(config-if)#tunnel mode ipv6ip auto-tunnel`	Specifies an IPv4-compatible tunnel using an IPv4-compatible IPv6 address.
`Router(config-if)#exit`	Returns to global configuration mode.

Configuring ISATAP Tunnels

The **tunnel source** command used in this configuration of an ISATAP tunnel must point to an interface with an IPv4 address configured. The ISATAP IPv6 address and prefix (or prefixes) advertised are configured as for a native IPv6 interface. The IPv6 tunnel interface must be configured with a modified EUI-64 address because the last 32 bits in the interface identifier are constructed using the IPv4 tunnel source address.

`Router#configure terminal`	Enters global configuration mode.
`Router(config)#ipv6 unicast-routing`	Enables the forwarding of IPv6 unicast datagrams globally on the router.

`Router(config)#ip cef`	Enables CEFv4 globally on the router.
`Router(config)#ipv6 cef`	Enables CEFv6 globally on the router.
`Router(config)#interface tunnel0`	Moves to tunnel interface configuration mode.
`Router(config-if)#ipv6 address 2001:0Db8:6301::/64 eui-64`	Assigns an IPv6 address to this interface.
`Router(config-if)#no ipv6 nd suppress-ra`	Sending of IPv6 router advertisements is disabled by default on tunnel interfaces. This command re-enables the sending of IPv6 router advertisements to allow neighbor discovery and client auto-configuration.
`Router(config-if)#tunnel source serial 0/0`	Specifies the source interface type and number for the tunnel interface.
	NOTE: The interface type and number specified in the **tunnel source** command is configured with an IPv4 address only.
`Router(config-if)#tunnel mode ipv6ip isatap`	Specifies an IPv6 overlay tunnel using an ISATAP address.
`Router(config-if)#exit`	Returns to global configuration mode.

Verifying IPv6 Tunnel Configuration and Operation

`Router#show interfaces tunnel`	Displays tunnel interface information.
`Router#show interface tunnel 0`	Displays tunnel interface information for the specific tunnel 0.
`Router#ping 10.0.0.1`	Diagnoses basic network connectivity.
`Router#show ip route`	Displays current state of routing table.
`Router#show ip route 10.0.0.2`	Displays current state of specified route.

Implementing NAT-PT for IPv6

The following restrictions apply to NAT-PT for IPv6:

- NAT-PT is not supported in Cisco Express Forwarding.
- NAT-PT has limited Application Layer Gateway (ALG) support for ICMP, FTP, and DNS.

- NAT-PT has the same restrictions that apply to IPv4 NAT where NAT-PT does not provide end-to-end security and the NAT-PT router can be a single point of failure in the network.
- Users must decide whether to use Static NAT-PT operation, Dynamic NAT-PT operation, Port Address Translation (PAT), or IPv4-mapped operation.

Configuring Basic IPv6 to IPv4 Connectivity for NAT-PT for IPv6

NOTE: This step is required for NAT-PT to operate. For NAT-PT to be operational, it must be enabled on both the incoming and outgoing interfaces.

NOTE: An IPv6 prefix with a prefix length of 96 must be specified. This prefix can be a unique local unicast prefix, a subnet of your allocated IPv6 prefix, or an extra prefix obtained from your ISP.

NOTE: The NAT-PT prefix can be configured globally or with different IPv6 prefixes on different interfaces. Using a different prefix on several interfaces allows the NAT-PT router to support an IPv6 network with multiple exit points to IPv4 networks.

`Router#configure terminal`	Enters global configuration mode.
`Router(config)#ipv6 nat prefix 2001:0db8::/96`	Assigns an IPv6 prefix as a global NAT-PT prefix.
	NOTE: Matching destination prefixes in IPv6 packets are translated by NAT-PT.
`Router(config)#interface fastethernet 0/0`	Moves to interface configuration mode.
`Router(config-if)#ipv6 address 2001:0db8:yyyy:1::9/64`	Assigns an IPv6 address to the interface and enables IPv6 processing on the interface.
`Router(config-if)#ipv6 nat`	Enables NAT-PT on the interface.
`Router(config-if)#exit`	Returns to global configuration mode.
`Router(config)#interface fastethernet 0/1`	Moves to interface configuration mode.
`Router(config-if)#ip address 192.168.30.9 255.255.255.0`	Assigns an IP address and mask to the interface.
`Router(config-if)#ipv6 nat`	Enables NAT-PT on the interface.

Configuring IPv4-Mapped NAT-PT Connectivity

NOTE: This step is required for NAT-PT to operate. For NAT-PT to be operational, it must be enabled on both the incoming and outgoing interfaces.

Router#**configure terminal**	Enters global configuration mode.
Router(config)#**interface fastethernet 0/0**	Moves to interface configuration mode.
Router(config-if)#**ipv6 nat prefix 2001::/96 v4-mapped v4mapacl**	Enables source to send traffic from an IPv6 network to an IPv4 network without configuring IPv6 destination address mapping. The keyword **v4mapacl** refers to a named ACL. An IPv6 prefix could also have been used in place of the ACL.

NOTE: The **ipv6 nat prefix** *xxxxx* **v4-mapped** command can also be configured globally, as opposed to on a specific interface.

Configuring Mappings for IPv6 Hosts Accessing IPv4 Hosts

NOTE: This step is required for NAT-PT to operate. You can use either static or dynamic IPv6 to IPv4 address mappings.

Router#**configure terminal**	Enters global configuration mode.
Router(config)#**ipv6 nat v6v4 source 2001:0db8:yyyy:1::1 10.21.8.10**	Creates a static IPv6 to IPv4 address mapping.
	NOTE: Use a separate instance of the **ipv6 nat v6v4 source** command to create every required mapping.
Router(config)#**ipv6 nat v6v4 source list pt-list1 pool v4pool**	Creates a dynamic IPv6 to IPv4 address mapping. Packets with a source address that pass the ACL named **pt-list1** will be dynamically translated using global addresses from the pool named **v4pool**.

Router(config)#ipv6 nat v6v4 pool v4pool 10.21.8.1 10.21.8.10 prefix-length 24	Specifies a pool of IPv4 addresses (10.21.8.1-10) to be used by NAT-PT.
	NOTE: When using dynamic mappings for NAT-PT, you must assign a pool of IPv4 addresses to be used and define which packets are to be translated. You can use an access control list (ACL), prefix list, or route map to determine which packets are to be translated.
Router(config)#ipv6 nat translation udp-timeout 600	Sets the time after which NAT-PT translations time out. Time is measured in seconds. The default is 300 seconds.

NOTE: The use of the **ipv6 nat translation timeout** command is optional.

Configuring IPv6 Access Control Lists

Router(config)#ipv6 access-list pt-list1	Defines an IPv6 access list and enters IPv6 access list configuration mode.
Router(config-ipv6-acl)#permit ipv6 2001:0db8:bbbb:1::/64 any	Specifies permit conditions for the IPv6 ACL.

NOTE: IPv6 ACL names cannot contain a space or quotation mark, or begin with a numeral.

NOTE: The complete syntax for the **permit** and/or the **deny** command is

Router(config-ipv6-acl)#**permit/deny** *protocol* {*source-ipv6-prefix/ prefix length* | **any** | **host** *source-ipv6-address*} [*operator* [*port-number*]] {*destination-ipv6-prefix/prefix length* | **any** | **host** *destination-ipv6-address*}

NOTE: The *protocol* argument (in this example it was **ipv6**) can be one of the keywords **ahp**, **esp**, **icmp**, **ipv6**, **pcp**, **sctp**, **tcp**, or **udp**, or an integer in the range of 0–255 representing an IPv6 protocol number.

NOTE: The *source-ipv6-prefix/prefix length* and *destination-ipv6-prefix/prefix length* arguments specify the source and destination IPv6 network or class or networks about which to set the permit/deny conditions

NOTE: The **any** keyword is an abbreviation for the IPv6 prefix ::/0.

NOTE: The **host** *source-ipv6-address* keyword and argument combination specifies the source IPv6 host address about which to set permit/deny conditions.

The **host** *destination-ipv6-address* keyword and argument combination specifies the destination IPv6 host address about which to set permit/deny conditions.

Configuring Mappings for IPv4 Hosts Accessing IPv6 Hosts

NOTE: This step is optional for NAT-PT to operate. The dynamic address mappings include assigning a pool of IPv6 addresses and using an ACL, prefix list, or route map to define which packets are to be translated.

`Router#`**`configure terminal`**	Enters global configuration mode.
`Router(config)#`**`ipv6 nat v4v6 source 10.21.8.11 2001:0db8:yyyy::2`**	Creates a static IPv4 to IPv6 address mapping.
	NOTE: Use a separate instance of the ipv6 nat v4v6 source command to create every required mapping.
`Router(config)#`**`ipv6 nat v4v6 source list 1 pool v6pool`**	Creates a dynamic IPv4 to IPv6 address mapping. Packets with a source address that pass the ACL numbered 1 will be dynamically translated using global addresses from the pool named v6pool.
`Router(config)#`**`ipv6 nat v4v6 pool v6pool 2001:0db8:yyyy::1 2001:0db8:yyyy::2 prefix-length 128`**	Specifies a pool of IPv6 addresses to be used by NAT-PT.
`Router(config)#`**`access-list 1 permit 182.168.30 0 0.0.0.255`**	Specifies an entry in a standard IPv4 access list.

Configuring Port Address Translation for IPv6 to IPv4 Address Mappings

NOTE: In this step, multiple IPv6 addresses are mapped to a single IPv4 address or to a pool of IPv4 addresses. Use an ACL, prefix list, or route map to determine which packets are to be translated.

Router#**configure terminal**	Enters global configuration mode.
Router(config)#**ipv6 nat v6v4 source 2001:0db8:yyyy:1::1 10.21.8.10 overload**	Enables a dynamic IPv6 to IPv4 address overload mapping using an interface address.
Router(config)#**ipv6 nat v6v4 source list pt-list1 interface serial 0/0/0 overload**	Enables a dynamic IPv6 to IPv4 address overload mapping. IPv6 addresses meeting the conditions of the ACL named **pt-list1** will be translated into the IPv4 address assigned to interface serial 0/0/0.
Router(config)#**ipv6 nat v6v4 source list pt-list1 pool v4pool overload**	Enables a dynamic IPv6 to IPv4 address overload mapping. IPv6 addresses meeting the conditions of the ACL named **pt-list1** will be translated into the IPv4 addresses defined in the pool named **v4pool**.
Router(config)#**ipv6 nat v6v4 pool v4pool 10.21.8.1 10.21.8.10 prefix-length 24**	Defines the pool named **v4pool** that will be used in NAT-PT overload.
Router(config)#**ipv6 nat translation udp-timeout 600**	Sets the time after which NAT-PT translations time out. Time is measured in seconds. Default is 86400 seconds (24 hours).

Verifying NAT-PT Configuration and Operation

Router#**clear ipv6 nat translation ***	Clears dynamic NAT-PT translations from the dynamic translation state table. The keyword * (star) is used to clear all dynamic NAT-PT translations.
	NOTE: Static translation configuration is not affected by this command.

`Router#`**`debug ipv6 nat`**	Displays debugging messages for NAT-PT translation events.
`Router#`**`debug ipv6 nat detailed`**	Displays detailed information about NAT-PT translation events.
`Router#`**`debug ipv6 nat port`**	Displays port allocation events.
`Router#`**`show ipv6 nat statistics`**	Displays NAT-PT statistics.
`Router#`**`show ipv6 nat translations`**	Displays active NAT-PT translations.
`Router#`**`show ipv6 nat translations verbose`**	Displays additional information for each translation table entry, including how long ago the entry was created and used.

Static Routes in IPv6

Figure 7-4 shows the network topology for the configuration that follows, which demonstrates how to configure static routes with IPv6.

Figure 7-4   Network Topology for IPv6 Static Routes

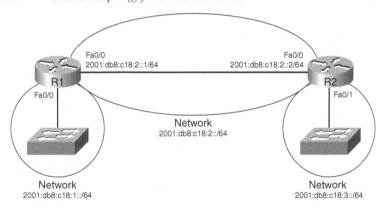

`R1(config)#`**`ipv6 route 2001:db8:c18:3::/64`** **`2001:db8:c18:2::2/64`**	Creates a static route configured to send all packets to a next-hop address of 2001:db8:c18:2::2.
`R1(config)#`**`ipv6 route 2001:db8:c18:3::/64`** **`fastethernet 0/0`**	Creates a directly attached static route configured to send packets out interface FastEthernet 0/0.
`R1(config)#`**`ipv6 route 2001:db8:c18:3::/64`** **`fastethernet 0/0 2001:db8:c18:2::2`**	Creates a fully specified static route on a broadcast interface.

Floating Static Routes in IPv6

R1(config)#**ipv6 route 2001:db8:c18:3::/64 fastethernet 0/0 200**	Creates a static route with an administrative distance (AD) set to 200, as opposed to a default AD of 1.
	NOTE: The default ADs used in IPv4 are the same for IPv6.

Verifying and Troubleshooting IPv6

Router#**clear ipv6 route ***	Deletes all routes from the IPv6 routing table.
	NOTE: Clearing all routes from the routing table will cause high CPU utilization rates as the routing table is rebuilt.
Router#**clear ipv6 route 2001:db8:c18:3::/64**	Clears this specific route from the IPv6 routing table.
Router#**clear ipv6 traffic**	Resets IPv6 traffic counters.
Router#**debug ipv6 cef {drop I events I hash I receive I table}**	Displays debug messages for all CEFv6 and dCEFv6 packets as specified by the keywords **drop, events, hash, receive,** or **table.**
	CAUTION: Using the **debug** command can severely affect router performance and can even cause the router to reboot. Caution should always be taken when using the **debug** command. Do not leave **debug** on. Use it long enough to gather needed information, and then disable debugging with the **undebug all** command.
Router#**debug ipv6 ospf adjacencies**	Displays debug messages about the OSPF adjacency process.
Router#**debug ipv6 packet**	Displays debug messages for IPv6 packets.

	TIP: Send your **debug** output to a syslog server to ensure that you have a copy of it in case your router is overloaded and needs to reboot.
`Router#debug ipv6 routing`	Displays debug messages for IPv6 routing table updates and route cache updates.
`Router#show ipv6 cef`	Displays entries in the IPv6 Forwarding Information Base (FIB).
`Router#show ipv6 cef summary`	Displays a summary of the entries in the IPv6 FIB.
`Router#show ipv6 interface`	Displays the status of interfaces configured for IPv6.
`Router#show ipv6 interface brief`	Displays a summarized status of interfaces configured for IPv6.
`Router#show ipv6 neighbors`	Displays IPv6 neighbor discovery cache information.
`Router#show ipv6 ospf`	Displays general information about the OSPFv3 routing process.
`Router#show ipv6 ospf border-routers`	Displays the internal OSPF routing table entries to an ABR or Autonomous System Boundary Router (ASBR).
`Router#show ipv6 ospf database`	Displays OSPFv3-related database information.
`Router#show ipv6 ospf database database-summary`	Displays how many of each type of link-state advertisement (LSA) exist for each area in the database.
`Router#show ipv6 ospf interface`	Displays OSPFv3-related interface information.

`Router#show ipv6 ospf neighbor`	Displays OSPFv3-related neighbor information.
`Router#show ipv6 ospf virtual-links`	Displays parameters and the current state of OSPFv3 virtual links.
`Router#show ipv6 protocols`	Displays the parameters and current state of the active IPv6 routing protocol processes.
`Router#show ipv6 route`	Displays the current IPv6 routing table.
`Router#show ipv6 route summary`	Displays a summarized form of the current IPv6 routing table.
`Router#show ipv6 routers`	Displays IPv6 router advertisement information received from other routers.
`Router#show ipv6 static`	Displays only static IPv6 routes installed in the routing table.
`Router#show ipv6 static 2001:db8:5555:0/16`	Displays only static route information about the specific address given.
`Router#show ipv6 static interface s0/0`	Displays only static route information with the specified interface as the outgoing interface.
`Router#show ipv6 static detail`	Displays a more detailed entry for IPv6 static routes.
`Router#show ipv6 traffic`	Displays statistics about IPv6 traffic.
`Router#show ipv6 tunnel`	Displays IPv6 tunnel information.

IPv6 Ping

`Router#`**`ping ipv6 2001:db8::3/64`**	Diagnoses basic network connectivity using IPv6 to the specified address.

NOTE: The following table lists the characters that can be displayed as output when using ping in IPv6.

Character	Description
!	Receipt of a reply.
.	Network server timed out while waiting for a reply.
?	Unknown error.
@	Unreachable for unknown reason.
A	Administratively unreachable. This usually means that an access control list (ACL) is blocking traffic.
B	Packet too big.
H	Host unreachable.
N	Network unreachable (beyond scope).
P	Port unreachable.
R	Parameter problem.
T	Time exceeded.
U	No route to host.

This chapter provides information and commands concerning the following topics:

- Verifying existing services
  - Network Address Translation
  - Dynamic Host Control Protocol
  - Access control lists and firewalls
  - Policy-based routing and Web Cache Communication Protocol
  - Hot Standby Router Protocol
- Configuration example: DSL using PPPoE
  - Configure PPoE (External Modem)
  - Configure the Dialer Interface
  - Define Interesting Traffic and Specify Default Routing
  - Configure NAT Using an ACL
  - Configure NAT Using a Route Map
  - Configure DHCP Service
  - Apply NAT Programming
  - Verify a PPPoE Connection
- Configuring PPPoA
- Connecting a teleworker to a branch office VPN using CLI
- Configuring IPsec site-to-site VPNs using CLI
- Configuring GRE tunnels over IPsec

Verifying Existing Services

Before a branch office or mobile worker is added into your network, you must first verify different services that already exist in your network. Without verifying what is currently happening in your network, you run the risk of affecting communication on your existing network or opening up a security hole for the sake of the new addition.

Network Address Translation

Router#**show ip nat statistics**	Displays Network Address Translation (NAT) statistics.
Router#**show ip nat translations**	Displays active NAT translations.
Router#**clear ip nat statistics**	Clears NAT statistics from buffers.
Router#**clear ip nat translations**	Clears active NAT translations.

Dynamic Host Control Protocol

Router#**show ip dhcp pool** [*name*]	Displays pool of inside local addresses assigned.
Router#**show ip dhcp server statistics**	Displays current statistics for the Dynamic Host Control Protocol (DHCP) server.

Access Control Lists and Firewalls

Router#**show ip interface**	Displays information about all interfaces on the device.
Router#**show ip interface serial 0/0/0**	Displays information about specific interface serial 0/0/0.
Router#**show access-lists**	Displays information about all access control lists (ACL) on this device.
Router#**show ip inspect interfaces**	Identifies interfaces that belong to classical IOS firewall configurations—Context-Based Access Control (CBAC).
Router#**show zone-pair security**	Identifies interfaces involved in zone-based firewalls.

Policy-Based Routing and Web Cache Communication Protocol

Router#**show ip policy**	Displays all policies configured on this device.
Router#**show ip interface**	Verifies where policies are attached.
Router#**show route-map**	Displays syntax of all route maps, including next-hop locations and any other redirection settings.

Hot Standby Router Protocol

Router#**show standby**	Displays all Hot Standby Router Protocol (HSRP) settings.
Router#**show standby brief**	Displays a summary of HSRP settings.
Router#**show standby fastethernet 0/0**	Displays information specific to interface FastEthernet 0/0.
Router#**show standby fastethernet 0/0 10**	Displays information specific to interface FastEthernet 0/0 and group 10.

Configuration Example: DSL Using PPPoE

Figure 8-1 shows an asymmetric digital subscriber line (ADSL) connection to the ISP DSL address multiplexer.

Figure 8-1   PPPoE Reference

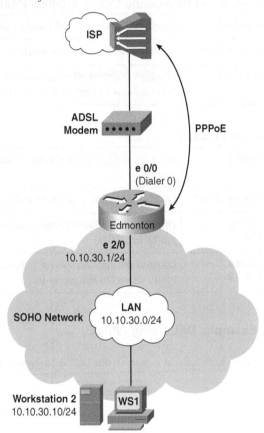

The programming steps for configuring Point-to-Point Protocol over Ethernet (PPPoE) on an Ethernet interface are as follows:

Step 1.   Configure PPPoE (external modem).

Step 2.   Configure the dialer interface.

Step 3.   Define interesting traffic and specify default routing.

Step 4.   Configure Network Address Translation (NAT) using an access control list (ACL).

Step 5.   Configure NAT using a route map.

Step 6.   Configure DHCP service.

Step 7.   Apply NAT programming.

Step 8.   Verify a PPPoE connection.

Step 1: Configure PPPoE (External Modem)

`Edmonton(config)#interface ethernet 0/0`	Enters interface configuration mode.
`Edmonton(config-if)#pppoe enable`	Enables PPPoE on the interface.
`Edmonton(config-if)#pppoe-client dial-pool-number 1`	Chooses the physical Ethernet interface for the PPPoE client dialer interface.
`Edmonton(config-if)#no shutdown`	Enables the interface.
`Edmonton(config-if)#exit`	Returns to global configuration mode.

Virtual Private Dial-Up Network (VPDN) Programming

`Edmonton(config)#vpdn enable`	Enables VPDN sessions on the network access server.
`Edmonton(config)#vpdn-group PPPOE-GROUP`	Creates a VPDN group and assigns it a unique name.
`Edmonton(config-vpdn)#request-dialin`	Initiates a dial-in tunnel.
`Edmonton(config-vpdn-req-in)#protocol pppoe`	Specifies the tunnel protocol.
`Edmonton(config-vpdn-req-in)#exit`	Exits request-dialin mode.
`Edmonton(config-vpdn)#exit`	Exits vpdn mode and returns to global configuration mode.

NOTE: VPDNs are legacy dial-in access services provided by ISPs to enterprise customers who chose not to purchase, configure, or maintain access servers or modem pools. A VPDN tunnel was built using Layer 2 Forwarding (L2F), Layer 2 Tunneling Protocol (L2TP), Point-to-Point Tunneling Protocol (PPTP), or Point-to-Point over Ethernet (PPPoE). The tunnel used UDP port 1702 to carry encapsulated PPP datagrams and control messages between the endpoints. Routers with Cisco IOS Release 12.2(13)T or earlier require the additional VPDN programming.

Step 2: Configure the Dialer Interface

`Edmonton(config)#interface dialer0`	Enters interface configuration mode.
`Edmonton(config-if)#ip address negotiated`	Obtains IP address via PPP/IPCP address negotiation.
`Edmonton(config-if)#ip mtu 1492`	Accommodates for the 6octet PPPoE header to eliminate fragmentation in the frame.
`Edmonton(config-if)#ip tcp adjust-mss 1452`	Adjusts the maximum segment size (MSS) of TCP SYN packets going through a router to eliminate fragmentation in the frame.
`Edmonton(config-if)#encapsulation ppp`	Enables PPP encapsulation on the dialer interface.
`Edmonton(config-if)#dialer pool 1`	Links the dialer interface with the physical interface Ethernet 0/1.
	NOTE: The ISP defines the type of authentication to use.

For Password Authentication Protocol (PAP)

`Edmonton(config-if)#ppp authentication pap callin`	Uses PAP for authentication.
`Edmonton(config-if)#ppp pap sent-username pieman password bananacream`	Enables outbound PAP user authentication with a username of **pieman** and a password of **bananacream**.

For Challenge Handshake Authentication Protocol (CHAP)

Edmonton(config-if)#**ppp authentication chap callin**	Enables outbound CHAP user authentication.
Edmonton(config-if)#**ppp chap hostname pieman**	Submits the CHAP username.
Edmonton(config-if)#**ppp chap password bananacream**	Submits the CHAP password.
Edmonton(config-if)#**exit**	Exits programming level.

Step 3: Define Interesting Traffic and Specify Default Routing

Edmonton(config)#**dialer-list 2 protocol ip permit**	Declares which traffic will invoke the dialing mechanism.
Edmonton(config)#**interface dialer0**	Enters interface configuration mode.
Edmonton(config-if)#**dialer-group 2**	Applies the "interesting traffic" rules in **dialer-list 2**.
Edmonton(config)#**ip route 0.0.0.0 0.0.0.0 dialer0**	Specifies the dialer0 interface as the candidate default next-hop address.

Step 4a: Configure NAT Using an ACL

Edmonton(config)#**access-list 1 permit 10.10.30.0 0.0.0.255**	Specifies an access control entry (ACE) for NAT.
Edmonton(config)#**ip nat pool NAT-POOL 192.31.7.1 192.31.7.2 netmask 255.255.255.0**	Defines the inside global (WAN side) NAT pool with subnet mask.
	NOTE: When a range of public addresses is used for the NAT/PAT inside global (WAN) addresses, it is defined by an address pool and called in the NAT definition programming.

`Edmonton(config)#ip nat inside source list 1` `pool NAT-POOL overload`	Specifies the NAT inside local addresses by ACL and the inside global addresses by address pool for the NAT process.
	NOTE: In the case where the inside global (WAN) address is dynamically assigned by the ISP, the outbound WAN interface is named in the NAT definition programming.
`Edmonton(config)#ip nat inside source list 1` `interface dialer0 overload`	Specifies the NAT inside local addresses (LAN) and inside global addresses (WAN) for the NAT process.

Step 4b: Configure NAT Using a Route Map

`Edmonton(config)#access-list 3` `permit 10.10.30.0 0.0.0.255`	Specifies the access control entry (ACE) for NAT.
	NOTE: The **route-map** command is typically used when redistributing routes from one routing protocol into another or to enable policy routing. The most commonly used method for defining the traffic to be translated in the NAT process is to use an ACL to choose traffic and call the ACL directly in the NAT programming. When used for NAT, a route map allows you to match any combination of ACL, next-hop IP address, and output interface to determine which pool to use. The Cisco Router and Security Device Manager (SDM) uses a route map to select traffic for NAT.
`Edmonton(config)#route-map` `ROUTEMAP permit 1`	Declares route map name and enters route-map mode.

Edmonton(config-route-map)#**match ip address 3**	Specifies the ACL that defines the dialer "interesting traffic."
Edmonton(config-route-map)#**exit**	Exits route-map mode.
Edmonton(config)#**ip nat inside source route-map ROUTEMAP interface dialer0 overload**	Specifies the NAT inside local (as defined by the route map) and inside global (interface dialer0) linkage for the address translation.

Step 5: Configure DHCP Service

Edmonton(config)#**ip dhcp excluded-address 10.10.30.1 10.10.30.5**	Excludes an IP address range from being offered by the router's DHCP service.
Edmonton(config)#**ip dhcp pool CLIENT-30**	Enters dhcp-config mode for the pool CLIENT-30.
Edmonton(dhcp-config)#**network 10.10.30.0 255.255.255.0**	Defines the IP network address.
Edmonton(dhcp-config)#**default-router 10.10.30.1**	Declares the router's vlan10 interface address as a gateway address.
Edmonton(dhcp-config)#**import all**	Imports DHCP option parameters into the DHCP server database from external DHCP service.
	NOTE: Any manually configured DHCP option parameters override the equivalent imported DHCP option parameters. Because they are obtained dynamically, these imported DHCP option parameters are not part of the router configuration and are not saved in NVRAM.

`Edmonton(dhcp-config)#dns-server 10.10.30.2`	Declares any required DNS server address(es).
`Edmonton(dhcp-config)#exit`	Exits dhcp-config mode.

Step 6: Apply NAT Programming

`Edmonton(config)#interface ethernet2/0`	Enters interface configuration mode.
`Edmonton(config-if)#ip nat inside`	Specifies the interface as an inside local (LAN side) interface.
`Edmonton(config)#interface dialer0`	Enters interface configuration mode.
`Edmonton(config-if)#ip nat outside`	Specifies the interface as an inside global (WAN side) interface.
`Edmonton(config-if)#end`	Returns to privileged EXEC mode.

Step 7: Verify a PPPoE Connection

`Edmonton#debug pppoe events`	Displays PPPoE protocol messages about events that are part of normal session establishment or shutdown.
`Edmonton#debug ppp authentication`	Displays authentication protocol messages such as CHAP and PAP messages.
`Edmonton#show pppoe session`	Displays information about currently active PPPoE sessions.
`Edmonton#show ip dhcp binding`	Displays address bindings on the Cisco IOS DHCP server.
`Edmonton#show ip nat translations`	Displays active NAT translations.

Configuring PPPoA

The programming steps for configuring PPP over ATM (PPPoA) on an ATM interface are as follows:

Step 1.   Configure PPPoA on the WAN interface (using subinterfaces).

Step 2.   Configure the dialer interface.

Step 3.   Verify a PPPoA connection.

NOTE: The remaining programming is the same as the PPPoE programming.

Step 1: Configure PPPoA on the WAN Interface (Using Subinterfaces)

`Edmonton(config)#interface atm0/0`	Enters interface configuration mode.
`Edmonton(config-if)#bundle-enable`	Enables multiple PVCs on the interface.
`Edmonton(config-if)#dsl operating-mode auto`	Automatically detects the DSL modulation scheme that the ISP is using.
`Edmonton(config-if)#interface atm0/0.1 pointtopoint`	Creates virtual ATM point-to-point subinterface.
`Edmonton(config-if)#pvc 1/2`	Assigns virtual circuit (VC) 2 on virtual path 1 to the subinterface.
	NOTE: pvc 1/2 is an example value that must be changed to match the value used by the ISP.
`Edmonton(config-if)#dialer pool-member 1`	Links the ATM interface to the dialer interface.
`Edmonton(config-if)#encapsulation aal5mux`	Configures the ATM adaptation layer (AAL) for multiplex (MUX)-type VCs.
	NOTE: The global default encapsulation option is aal5snap.

Step 2: Configure the Dialer Interface

`Edmonton(config)#`**`interface dialer0`**	Enters interface configuration mode.
	NOTE: When configuring the dialer interface in an ATM environment, it is not necessary to configure the maximum transmission unit (MTU) and adjust the MSS. This is required only when configuring PPPoE.
`Edmonton(config-if)#`**`ip address negotiated`**	Obtains IP address via PPP/IPCP address negotiation.
`Edmonton(config-if)#`**`encapsulation ppp`**	Enables PPP encapsulation on the dialer interface.
`Edmonton(config-if)#`**`dialer pool 1`**	Links the dialer interface with the physical interface ATM 0/0.

For Password Authentication Protocol (PAP)

`Edmonton(config-if)#`**`ppp authentication pap callin`**	Uses PAP for authentication.
`Edmonton(config-if)#`**`ppp pap sent-username pieman password bananacream`**	Enables outbound PAP user authentication.

For Challenge Handshake Authentication Protocol (CHAP)

`Edmonton(config-if)#`**`ppp authentication chap callin`**	Enables outbound CHAP user authentication.
`Edmonton(config-if)#`**`ppp chap hostname pieman`**	Submits the CHAP username.
`Edmonton(config-if)#`**`ppp chap password bananacream`**	Submits the CHAP password.
`Edmonton(config-if)#`**`exit`**	Returns to global configuration mode.

Step 3: Verify a PPPoA Connection

Edmonton#**debug pppatm event vc 1/2**	Displays events on virtual circuit 2 on virtual path 1.
Edmonton#**debug pppatm error vc 1/2**	Displays errors on virtual circuit 2 on virtual path 1.
Edmonton#**show atm interface atm0/0**	Displays ATM-specific information about an ATM interface.
Edmonton#**show dsl interface atm0/0.1**	Displays information specific to the ADSL for a specified ATM interface.
Edmonton#**debug ppp authentication**	Displays authentication protocol messages such as CHAP and PAP messages.
Edmonton#**show ip dhcp binding**	Displays address bindings on the Cisco IOS DHCP server.
Edmonton#**show ip nat translations**	Displays active NAT translations.

Configuring a Teleworker to a Branch Office VPN Using CLI

This section refers to Figure 8-2 and provides details about the configuration for the Edmonton router.

Figure 8-2   VPN Network Topology

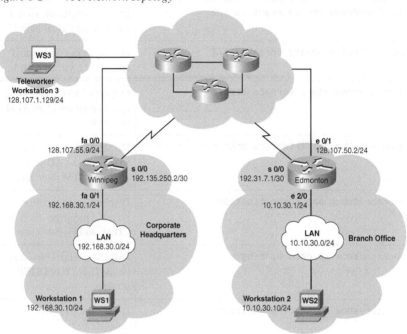

The following steps are used to configure the Edmonton router:

Step 1. Configure the Internet Security Association and Key Management Protocol (ISAKMP) policy (IKE phase 1).

Step 2. Configure policies for the client group(s).

Step 3. Configure the IPsec transform sets (IKE phase 2, tunnel termination).

Step 4. Configure router AAA and add VPN client users.

Step 5. Create VPN client policy for security association negotiation.

Step 6. Configure the crypto map (IKE phase 2).

Step 7. Apply the crypto map to the interface.

Step 8. Verify the VPN service.

Step 1: Configure the ISAKMP Policy (IKE Phase 1)

`Edmonton(config)#crypto isakmp policy 1`	Creates an IKE phase 1 policy.
`Edmonton(config-isakmp)#encryption 3des`	Selects 3DES as the encryption type.
`Edmonton(config-isakmp)#hash md5`	Selects MD5 as the hashing algorithm.
`Edmonton(config-isakmp)#authentication preshare`	Uses a preshared encryption key.
`Edmonton(config-isakmp)#group 2`	Uses Diffie-Hellman group 2 key exchange algorithm.
`Edmonton(config-isakmp)#exit`	Exits isakmp mode and returns to global configuration mode.

Step 2: Configure Policies for the Client Group(s)

`Edmonton(config)#crypto isakmp client configuration group VPNGROUP`	Creates a group for VPN clients.
`Edmonton(config-isakmp-group)#key 12345678`	Uses the key 12345678.
`Edmonton(config-isakmp-group)#pool VPNPOOL`	Uses addresses defined in the address pool VPNPOOL.
`Edmonton(config-isakmp-group)#dns 192.31.7.1`	Points the VPN client to a DNS service.
`Edmonton(config-isakmp-group)#wins 10.10.30.10`	Points the VPN client at a WINS service.
`Edmonton(config-isakmp-group)#exit`	Exits isakmp-group mode and returns to global configuration mode.

Step 3: Configure the IPsec Transform Sets (IKE Phase 2, Tunnel Termination)

Edmonton(config)#**crypto ipsec transform-set TRANSFORM-1 esp-3des esp-sha-hmac**	Creates a transform set for the IKE phase 2 policy.
Edmonton(cfg-crypto-trans)#**exit**	Exits cfg-crypto-trans mode.

Step 4: Configure Router AAA and Add VPN Client Users

Edmonton(config)#**aaa new-model**	Starts the router AAA service.
	NOTE: Cisco IOS–based VPNs require the router AAA service to be enabled. VPN client users can be defined locally in the router or on an AAA server. There are separate lists for authentication and authorization of VPN users.
Edmonton(config)#**aaa authentication login default local**	Verifies login authentication for the "default" group using the local user database.
Edmonton(config)#**aaa authentication login VPNAUTH local**	Verifies login authentication for the VPNAUTH group using the local user database.
Edmonton(config)#**aaa authorization exec default local**	Verifies EXEC authorization for the "default" group using the local user database.
Edmonton(config)#**aaa authorization network VPNAUTHOR local**	Verifies network access authorization for the VPNAUTHOR group using the local user database.

Edmonton(config)#**username user1 secret password1**	Creates user for VPN authentication.
Edmonton(config)#**username user2 secret password2**	Creates user for VPN authentication.

Step 5: Create VPN Client Policy for Security Association Negotiation

Edmonton(config)#**crypto dynamic-map DYNMAP 1**	Creates a dynamic crypto map.
Edmonton(config-crypto-map)#**set transform-set TRANSFORM-1**	Defines the transform set the client must match to.
Edmonton(config-crypto-map)#**reverse-route**	Has the router add a return route for the VPN client in the routing table.
Edmonton(config-crypto-map)#**exit**	Exits config-crypto-map mode.

Step 6: Configure the Crypto Map (IKE Phase 2)

Edmonton(config)#**crypto map CRYPTOMAP client authentication list VPNAUTH**	Configures IKE extended authentication (Xauth) for the VPN group VPNAUTH.
Edmonton(config)#**crypto map CRYPTOMAP isakmp authorization list VPNAUTHOR**	Configures IKE key lookup from a AAA server for the VPN group VPNAUTHOR.
Edmonton(config)#**crypto map CRYPTOMAP client configuration address respond**	Enables the router to accept IP address requests from any peer.
Edmonton(config)#**crypto map CRYPTOMAP 65535 ipsec-isakmp dynamic DYNMAP**	Uses IKE to establish IPsec security associations (SA) as specified by crypto map DYNMAP.

Step 7: Apply the Crypto Map to the Interface

`Edmonton(config)#`**`interface ethernet 2/0`**	Enters interface configuration mode.
`Edmonton(config-if)#`**`crypto map CRYPTOMAP`**	Applies the crypto map CRYPTOMAP.
`Edmonton(config-if)#`**`end`**	Exits to privileged mode.

Step 8: Verify the VPN Service

`Edmonton#`**`show crypto ipsec sa`**	Displays the settings used by current SAs.
`Edmonton#`**`show crypto isakmp sa`**	Displays current IKE SAs.
`Edmonton#`**`show crypto session`**	Displays status information for active crypto sessions.
`Edmonton#`**`show crypto dynamic-map`**	Displays a dynamic crypto map set.
`Edmonton#`**`show crypto map`**	Displays the crypto map configuration.
	NOTE: Before issuing a **debug** command, you should read the information for that command in the *Cisco IOS Debug Command Reference* for your IOS version to determine the impact on the device.
`Edmonton#`**`debug crypto ipsec`**	Displays IPsec.
`Edmonton#`**`debug crypto isakmp`**	Displays messages about IKE events.
`Edmonton#`**`debug crypto isakmp error`**	Displays error messages for IKE-related operations.
`Edmonton#`**`debug crypto ipsec error`**	Displays error messages for IPsec-related operations.

Configuring IPsec Site-to-Site VPNs Using CLI

This section refers to Figure 8-2 and provides details about the configuration for the Winnipeg router.

The programming steps for configuring the Winnipeg router are as follows:

Step 1. Configure the ISAKMP policy (IKE phase 1).

Step 2. Configure the IPsec transform sets (IKE phase 2, tunnel termination).

Step 3. Configure the crypto ACL (interesting traffic, secure data transfer).

Step 4. Configure the crypto map (IKE phase 2).

Step 5. Apply the crypto map to the interface (IKE phase 2).

Step 6. Configure the firewall interface ACL.

Step 7. Verify the VPN service.

Step 1: Configure the ISAKMP Policy (IKE Phase 1)

`Winnipeg(config)#`**`crypto isakmp policy 1`**	Creates an IKE policy.
`Winnipeg(config-isakmp)#`**`encryption 3des`**	Defines 3DES encryption.
`Winnipeg(config-isakmp)#`**`hash sha`**	Chooses sha as the hashing algorithm.
`Winnipeg(config-isakmp)#`**`authentication preshare`**	Specifies authentication with a preshared key.
`Winnipeg(config-isakmp)#`**`group 2`**	Specifies Diffie-Hellman group 2 key exchange algorithm.
`Winnipeg(config-isakmp)#`**`lifetime 86400`**	Specifies the lifetime of the IKE SA.
`Winnipeg(config-isakmp)#`**`exit`**	Exits isakmp configuration mode.
`Winnipeg(config)#`**`crypto isakmp key 12345678 address 192.31.7.1`**	Specifies the key required for the tunnel endpoint.
	NOTE: The VPN tunnel peer (Edmonton router) must have one IKE phase 1 policy that matches the IKE phase 1 policy in the Winnipeg router.

Step 2: Configure the IPsec Transform Sets (IKE Phase 2, Tunnel Termination)

`Winnipeg(config)#crypto ipsec transform-set` `TRANSFORM-0 esp-sha-hmac esp-3des`	Creates a transform set for the IKE phase 2 policy.
`Winnipeg(cfg-crypto-trans)#mode tunnel`	Encapsulates the entire datagram.
`Winnipeg(cfg-crypto-trans)#exit`	Exits cfg-crypto-trans mode.
`Winnipeg(config)#crypto ipsec security-` `association lifetime seconds 1200`	Defines a 20-minute SA lifetime.

Step 3: Configure the Crypto ACL (Interesting Traffic, Secure Data Transfer)

`Winnipeg#configure terminal`	Enters global configuration mode.
`Winnipeg(config)#access-list 100 permit ip` `192.168.30.0 0.0.0.255 10.10.30.0 0.0.0.255`	Defines the source and destination of traffic that will use the IPsec tunnel.

Step 4: Configure the Crypto Map (IKE Phase 2)

`Winnipeg(config)#crypto map CRYPTO-MAP-0 1` `ipsec-isakmp`	Defines the crypto map CRYPTO-MAP-0 to use IPsec with ISAKMP.
`Winnipeg(config-crypto-map)#set peer` `192.31.7.1`	Specifies the IP address of the VPN peer.
`Winnipeg(config-crypto-map)#set transform-set` `TRANSFORM-0`	Uses the transform set TRANSFORM-0 for IKE phase 2 policy.
`Winnipeg(config-crypto-map)#match address 100`	Defines the IP addresses for the IPsec tunnel.
`Winnipeg(config-crypto-map)#exit`	Exits crypto-map configuration mode.

NOTE: The Edmonton tunnel termination router has the following mirrored programming: tunnel peer IP address, interesting traffic ACL, and firewall ACL permitting VPN protocols.

Edmonton(config)#`access-list 101 permit ip` `10.10.30.0 0.0.0.255 192.168.30.1 0.0.0.255`	Defines the source and destination IP addresses of the VPN traffic.
Edmonton(config-crypto-map)#`match address 101`	Defines the IP addresses for the IPsec tunnel.
Edmonton(config-crypto-map)#`set peer` `128.107.55.9`	Specifies the IP address of the IPsec peer.
Edmonton(config)#`access-list 120 permit ahp` `host 128.107.55.9 host 192.31.7.1`	Permits VPN protocol: Authentication Header (AH).
Edmonton(config)#`access-list 120 permit esp` `host 128.107.55.9 host 192.31.7.1`	Permits VPN protocol: Encapsulating Security Payload (ESP).
Edmonton(config)#`access-list 120 permit udp` `host 128.107.55.9 host 192.31.7.1 eq isakmp`	Permits VPN protocol: ISAKMP.

Step 5: Apply the Crypto Map to the Interface (IKE Phase 2)

Winnipeg(config)#`interface fastethernet 0/0`	Enters interface configuration mode.
Winnipeg(config-if)#`crypto map CRYPTO-MAP-0`	Applies the crypto map at the terminating interface.
Winnipeg(config-if)#`exit`	Exits interface configuration mode.

Step 6: Configure the Firewall Interface ACL

Winnipeg(config)#`access-list 120 permit ahp` `host 192.31.7.1 host 128.107.55.9`	Permits VPN protocol: AH.
Winnipeg(config)#`access-list 120 permit esp` `host 192.31.7.1 host 128.107.55.9`	Permits VPN protocol: ESP.

`Winnipeg(config)#access-list 120 permit udp host 192.31.7.1 host 128.107.55.9 eq isakmp`	Permits VPN protocol: ISAKMP.
	NOTE: The ACL permitting VPN protocols is applied inbound at the border router or firewall WAN interface.
`Winnipeg(config)#interface fastethernet 0/0`	Enters interface configuration mode.
`Winnipeg(config-if)#ip access-group 120 in`	Applies VPN protocol ACL inbound at the local terminating interface.

Step 7: Verify the VPN Service

`Winnipeg#show crypto ipsec sa`	Displays the settings used by current SAs.
`Winnipeg#show crypto isakmp sa`	Displays current IKE SAs.
`Winnipeg#show crypto session`	Displays status information for active crypto sessions.
`Winnipeg#show crypto dynamic-map`	Displays a dynamic crypto map set.
`Winnipeg#show crypto map`	Displays the crypto map configuration.
`Winnipeg#debug crypto ipsec`	Displays IPsec events.
`Winnipeg#debug crypto isakmp`	Displays messages about IKE events.
`Winnipeg#debug crypto isakmp error`	Displays error messages for IKE-related operations.
`Winnipeg#debug crypto ipsec error`	Displays error messages for IPsec-related operations.

Configuring GRE Tunnels over IPsec

This section refers to Figure 8-2 and provides details about the configuration of a GRE over IPsec tunnel, in this case from Winnipeg to Edmonton.

The programming steps for configuring the Winnipeg router are as follows:

Step 1.   Create the GRE tunnel.

Step 2.   Specify the IPsec VPN authentication method.

Step 3.   Specify the IPsec VPN IKE proposals.

Step 4.   Specify the IPsec VPN transform sets.

Step 5.   Specify static routing for the GRE over IPsec tunnel.

Step 6.   Specify routing with OSPF for the GRE over IPsec tunnel.

Step 7.   Enable the crypto programming at the interfaces.

NOTE: The Winnipeg and Edmonton routers are programmed to provide connectivity for LAN and WAN, including any public to private IP translation.

Step 1: Create the GRE Tunnel

`Winnipeg(config)#interface tunnel0`	Enters interface configuration mode (virtual GRE tunnel interface).
`Winnipeg(config-if)#ip address 192.168.3.1 255.255.255.0`	Assigns the tunnel IP address and netmask.
`Winnipeg(config-if)#tunnel source fastethernet 0/0`	Defines the local tunnel interface.
`Winnipeg(config-if)#tunnel destination 192.31.7.1`	Programs the far-end tunnel IP.
	NOTE: The peer termination router has mirrored programming with "tunnel destination 128.107.55.9."
`Winnipeg(config-if)#no shutdown`	Turns on the tunnel interface.

Step 2: Specify the IPsec VPN Authentication Method

`Winnipeg#`**`configure terminal`**	Enters global configuration mode.
`Winnipeg(config)#`**`crypto isakmp policy 10`**	Creates an IKE phase 1 policy.
`Winnipeg(config-isakmp)#`**`authentication preshare`**	Specifies use of a preshared encryption key.
`Winnipeg(config-isakmp)#`**`encryption 3des`**	Specifies use of 3DES encryption.
`Winnipeg(config-isakmp)#`**`group 2`**	Specifies use of the Diffie-Hellman group 2 hashing algorithm.
`Winnipeg(config-isakmp)#`**`exit`**	Exits isakmp configuration mode.
`Winnipeg(config)#`**`crypto isakmp key 12345678`** **`address 192.31.7.1`**	Specifies the key required for the tunnel endpoint.
`Edmonton(config)#`**`crypto isakmp key 12345678`** **`address 128.107.55.9`**	Specifies the key required for the tunnel endpoint.
	NOTE: The peer termination router must have the same key and IP address of its peer termination router (128.107.55.9).

Step 3: Specify the IPsec VPN IKE Proposals

`Winnipeg(config)#`**`access-list 101 permit gre`** **`host 128.107.55.9 host 192.31.7.1`**	Allows GRE protocol traffic between GRE tunnel endpoints.
`Winnipeg(config)#`**`crypto map VPN-1 10 ipsec-isakmp`**	Defines the crypto map VPN-1 to use IPsec with ISAKMP.
`Winnipeg(config-crypto-map)#`**`set peer`** **`192.31.7.1`**	Specifies the IP address of the IPsec peer.

`Winnipeg(config-crypto-map)#`**`set transform-set`** **`TO-EDMONTON`**	Uses the transform set TO-EDMONTON for IKE phase 2 policy.
`Winnipeg(config-crypto-map)#`**`match address 101`**	Defines the IP addresses for the IPsec tunnel.
`Winnipeg(config-crypto-map)#`**`exit`**	Exits crypto-map configuration mode.
`Edmonton(config)#`**`access-list 102 permit gre`** **`host 192.31.7.1 host 128.107.55.9`**	Allows GRE protocol traffic between GRE tunnel endpoints.
`Edmonton(config-crypto-map)#`**`set peer`** **`128.107.55.9`**	Specifies the IP address of the IPsec peer.
`Edmonton(config-crypto-map)#`**`match address 102`**	Defines the IP addresses for the IPsec tunnel.
	NOTE: The Edmonton tunnel termination router has the following mirrored programming: ACL permitting GRE inbound from the Winnipeg router, tunnel peer, and interesting traffic ACL.

Step 4: Specify the IPsec VPN Transform Sets

`Winnipeg(config)#`**`crypto ipsec transform-set`** **`TO-EDMONTON esp-des esp-md5-hmac`**	Creates the transform set TO-EDMONTON for the IKE phase 2 policy.
`Winnipeg(cfg-crypto-trans)#`**`exit`**	Exits cfg-crypto-trans configuration mode.

Step 5a: Specify Static Routing for the GRE over IPsec Tunnel

Winnipeg(config)#`ip route 0.0.0.0 0.0.0.0` `128.107.55.10`	Configures a static default route to the physical next-hop IP address.
Winnipeg(config)#`ip route 10.10.30.0` `255.255.255.0 192.168.3.2`	Configures a static route for (local) tunnel traffic giving the far-end tunnel address as the next-hop IP address.

Step 5b: Specify Routing with OSPF for the GRE over IPsec Tunnel

Winnipeg(config)#`router ospf 1`	Enables OSPF with process ID 1.
Winnipeg(config-router)#`passive-interface` `fastethernet 0/0`	Disables OSPF routing updates on interface FastEthernet 0/0.
Winnipeg(config-router)#`passive-interface` `fastethernet 0/1`	Disables OSPF routing updates on interface FastEthernet 0/1.
	NOTE: Interface Tunnel0 is the only interface participating in OSPF.
Winnipeg(config-router)#`network 192.168.30.0` `0.0.0.255 area 0`	Configures 192.168.30.0/24 into OSPF area 0.
Winnipeg(config-router)#`network 192.168.3.0` `0.0.0.255 area 0`	Read this line to say, "Any interface with an address of 192.168.3.x is to be placed into area 0."
Winnipeg(config-router)#`exit`	Returns to global configuration mode.

NOTE: GRE is multiprotocol and can tunnel any OSI Layer 3 protocol.

Step 6: Enable the Crypto Programming at the Interfaces

`Winnipeg(config-if)#`**`interface`** **`fastethernet 0/0`**	Enters interface configuration mode.
`Winnipeg(config-if)#`**`shutdown`**	Turns the interface off.
`Winnipeg(config-if)#`**`crypto map VPN-1`**	Applies the crypto map to the WAN interface.
`Winnipeg(config-if)#`**`no shutdown`**	Turns the interface on.
`Winnipeg(config-if)#`**`exit`**	Returns to global configuration mode.
`Winnipeg(config)#`**`interface tunnel0`**	Enters interface configuration mode.
`Winnipeg(config-if)#`**`shutdown`**	Turns the interface off.
`Winnipeg(config-if)#`**`crypto map VPN-1`**	Applies the crypto map to the tunnel interface.
`Winnipeg(config-if)#`**`no shutdown`**	Turns the interface on.

Create Your Own Journal Here

Even though I have tried to be as complete as possible in this reference guide, invariably I will have left something out that you need in your specific day-to-day activities. That is why this section is here. Use these blank lines to enter in your own notes, making this reference guide your own personalized journal.

GO FURTHER, FASTER. BECOME CERTIFIED.

Stop thinking about your potential. Realize it. Take your training, skills and knowledge to the next level. Get Cisco Certified through Pearson VUE.

Take your Cisco Career Certification exam at one of more than 4,400 conveniently located Pearson VUE® Authorized Test Centers worldwide to experience a no-hassle test experience. To register at a test center near you, simply visit PearsonVUE.com/Cisco.

PEARSON
VUE